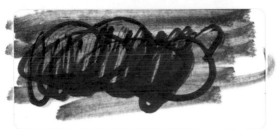

A BASIC GUIDE TO

Decathlon

An Official U.S. Olympic Committee Sports Series

The U.S. Olympic Committee

Griffin Publishing Group

This Hardcover Edition Distributed By
Gareth Stevens Publishing
A World Almanac Education Group Company

This hardcover edition distributed by
Gareth Stevens Publishing
A World Almanac Education Group Company
330 West Olive Street, Suite 100
Milwaukee, WI 53212 USA

For a free color catalog describing Gareth Stevens' list of high-quality books and multimedia programs, call 1-800-542-2595 (USA) or 1-800-461-9120 (Canada). Gareth Stevens Publishing's Fax: (414) 332-3567.
Visit Gareth Stevens' website at: www.garethstevens.com

Library of Congress Cataloging-in-Publication Data for this hardcover edition available upon request from Gareth Stevens Publishing. Fax: (414) 336-0157 for the attention of the Publishing Records Department.

Hardcover edition: ISBN 0-8368-2796-1

Editorial Statement
In the interest of brevity, the Editors have chosen to use the standard English form of address. Please be advised that this usage is not meant to suggest a restriction to, nor an endorsement of, any individual or group of individuals, either by age, gender, or athletic ability. The Editors certainly acknowledge that boys and girls, men and women, of every age and physical condition are actively involved in sports, and we encourage everyone to enjoy the sports of his or her choice.

1 2 3 4 5 6 7 8 9 05 04 03 02 01
Printed in the United States of America

ACKNOWLEDGMENTS

PUBLISHER	Griffin Publishing Group
DIR. / OPERATIONS	Robin L. Howland
PROJECT MANAGER	Bryan K. Howland
WRITER	Frank Zarnowski, Ph.D.
BOOK DESIGN	m2design group
USOC CHAIRMAN/PRESIDENT	William J. Hybl
EDITORS	Geoffrey M. Horn
	Catherine Gardner
CONTRIBUTING EDITORS	Barry King
	Mark Davis
PHOTOS	Dan O'Brien Youth Foundation
	Frank Zarnowski, Ph.D.
	Millsport
COVER DESIGN	m2design group
COVER ATHLETE	Dan O'Brien
COVER PHOTO	Tim Defrisco

Special thanks to USA Track and Field for the athlete biographical information.

The United States Olympic Committee

The U.S. Olympic Committee (USOC) is the custodian of the U.S. Olympic Movement and is dedicated to providing opportunities for American athletes of all ages.

The USOC, a streamlined organization of member organizations, is the moving force for support of sports in the United States that are on the program of the Olympic and/or Pan American Games, or those wishing to be included.

The USOC has been recognized by the International Olympic Committee since 1894 as the sole agency in the United States whose mission involves training, entering, and underwriting the full expenses for the United States teams in the Olympic and Pan American Games. The USOC also supports the bid of U.S. cities to host the winter and summer Olympic Games, or the winter and summer Pan American Games, and after reviewing all the candidates, votes on and may endorse one city per event as the U.S. bid city. The USOC also approves the U.S. trial sites for the Olympic and Pan American Games team selections.

Welcome to the Olympic Sports Series

We feel this unique series will encourage parents, athletes of all ages, and novices who are thinking about a sport for the first time to get involved with the challenging and rewarding world of Olympic sports.

This series of Olympic sport books covers both summer and winter sports, features Olympic history and basic sports fundamentals, and encourages family involvement. Each book includes information on how to get started in a particular sport, including equipment and clothing; rules of the game; health and fitness; basic first aid; and guidelines for spectators. Of special interest is the information on opportunities for senior citizens, volunteers, and physically challenged athletes. In addition, each book is enhanced by photographs and illustrations and a complete, easy-to-understand glossary.

Because this family-oriented series neither assumes nor requires prior knowledge of a particular sport, it can be enjoyed by all age groups. Regardless of anyone's level of sports knowledge, playing experience, or athletic ability, this official U.S. Olympic Committee Sports Series will encourage understanding and participation in sports and fitness.

The purchase of these books will assist the U.S. Olympic Team. This series supports the Olympic mission and serves importantly to enhance participation in the Olympic and Pan American Games.

United States Olympic Committee

Contents

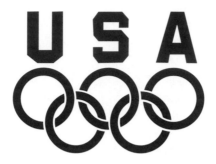

AN ATHLETE'S CREED

The most important thing in the Olympic Games is not to win but to take part, just as the most important thing in life is not the triumph but the struggle. The essential thing is not to have conquered but to have fought well.

These famous words, commonly referred to as the Olympic Creed, were once spoken by Baron Pierre de Coubertin, founder of the modern Olympic Games. Whatever their origins, they aptly describe the theme behind each and every Olympic competition.

Metric Equivalents

Wherever possible, measurements given are those specified by the Olympic rules. Other measurements are given in metric or standard U.S. units, as appropriate. For purposes of comparison, the following rough equivalents may be used.

1 kilometer (km)	= 0.62 mile (mi)	1 mi = 1.61 km
1 meter (m)	= 3.28 feet (ft)	1 ft = 0.305 m
	= 1.09 yards (yd)	1 yd = 0.91 m
1 centimeter (cm)	= 0.39 inch (in)	1 in = 2.54 cm
	= 0.1 hand	1 hand (4 in) = 10.2 cm
1 kilogram (kg)	= 2.2 pounds (lb)	1 lb = 0.45 kg
1 milliliter (ml)	= 0.03 fluid ounce (fl oz)	1 fl oz = 29.573 ml
1 liter	= 0.26 gallons (gal)	1 gal = 3.785 liters

1

The Decathlon in Olympic History

The Jim Thorpe Story

When King Gustav V of Sweden presented awards at the 1912 Olympic Games in Stockholm, he proclaimed to the decathlon winner, an American Indian named Jim Thorpe: "You, sir, are the world's greatest athlete." Jim is purported to have replied, "Thanks, King," to the Swedish monarch, a story, true or not, which itself which has become part of the Thorpe saga.

Ever since, the Olympic decathlon champion or world-record holder has been dubbed "The World's Greatest Athlete." And rightly so, since the decathlon is the only objective test of all-around athletic ability. Decathletes must contest ten separate events and have those performances tallied on a standard scoring table. The decathlon measures basic sporting abilities like jumping, sprinting, and throwing. Within the backdrop and rules of track and field, decathlon champions must exhibit the four S's: speed, spring, strength, and stamina.

Since 1912, great decathlon champions like Bob Mathias, Rafer Johnson, Bruce Jenner, Daley Thompson, and others have become household names. But they all owe much to the legend of Thorpe.

In 1912, Jim Thorpe, a Native American from the Sac and Fox tribe, was a student at the Carlisle (PA) Indian School and was already being called "the athletic marvel of the age." He was the nation's best football player. Then, turning his attention to the Stockholm Olympic Games, Jim made the U.S. Olympic Team in four events and won gold medals in the first Olympic decathlon and pentathlon.

Cumberland County Historical Society

Jim Thorpe, winner of the first Olympic decathlon crown in 1912

A year later he was stripped of his Olympic records and medals when it was discovered he had played professional baseball for a few dollars, not unusual for students of the day. But the Amateur Athletic Union (AAU) of the United States made an example of Thorpe, claiming he was not a true amateur. It was a raw deal, and Thorpe left Carlisle and became a professional athlete, playing major and minor league baseball for another ten seasons and professional football until 1929, when he was 41. Indeed, he was the first president of the National Football League (NFL). No one surpassed his decathlon score for 15 years. In 1950 he was voted the "Athlete of the First Half Century."

In 1982, 29 years after Thorpe's penniless death, the International Olympic Committee (IOC) restored his name to the Olympic record books. In January 1983, the IOC presented facsimile medals (the originals had been lost) to his children.

Thorpe's Native American heritage, remarkable ability, long professional career, and loss of Olympic medals elevated him to an almost mythical status. Even today, nine decades after his Stockholm triumph, his name, of all decathlon men, is still history's most recognized.

The Ancient Pentathlon

In one sense, modern decathlon history begins with the Thorpe story. Yet, in another sense, the story begins 26 centuries earlier. The Greeks created an all-around test, the pentathlon, for the ancient Olympic Games. The ancient pentathlon consisted of a long jump, discus throw, javelin throw, sprint, and wrestling match. There is still considerable academic debate pertaining to the order of events and how the winner was determined.

The Greeks invented the pentathlon to ascertain their best all-around athletes. Five (*penta*) seemed a convenient number to them, much like ten (*deca*) is to contemporaries. The Greek pentathlon

Source: F.A.M. Webster's *The Evolution of the Olympic Games, 1829 B.C. - 1914 A.D.*

An ancient Greek amphora depicts several of the pentathlon events: discus, long jump, and javelin.

demanded a blend of speed and strength. Technique and endurance played lesser roles. Much like the first day of the decathlon, the Greek pentathlon was power oriented. According to most evidence, wrestling was the last event, and only necessary if the pentathlon winner had not been determined in the earlier contests.

The pentathlon was introduced at Olympia in 708 B.C. and continued unabated every fourth year for almost 11 centuries. The first Olympic pentathlon winner was Lampis, a young Spartan. Although the Greeks did not keep records in a modern sense (in ancient Greek there is no way to say "break a record" or "set a record"), we do have the names of many of the pentathlon winners. For example we know that Gorgos, of the small town of Elis (near Olympia), won four ancient pentathlons.

The pentathlon was not just an Olympic event. By the sixth century B.C. major religious games were held in Corinth, Delphi, and Nemea. Secondary athletic festivals were conducted in most towns of the Greek world. Athletes could and did compete in numerous pentathlons annually.

The popularity of the pentathlon varied over time and from person to person. Some authorities, including Aristotle, had lofty respect for the pentathlete's combination of speed and strength. Others, like the philosopher Plato, also a wrestler (his name means "broad shouldered"), considered the pentathlete a mediocre performer. But the poet Bacchlylides, in an ode to the winner, leaves little doubt about his sentiment for Automedes, winner of a Nemean Games pentathlon.

> He shone among the other pentathletes as the bright moon in the middle of the month dims the radiance of the stars: even thus he showed his lovely body to the great ring of watching Greeks, as he threw the round discus and hurled the shaft of black leaved elder (javelin) from his grasp to the steep heights of heaven, and roused the cheers of the spectators by his lithe movements in the wrestling and the end.

Greek Olympians, including the pentathletes, were hardly amateurs in the modern sense. They were paid for their efforts, and by the fifth century B.C. city-states bid for the services of athletes and generously rewarded them for major victories. Today's most authoritative scholar on the ancient Olympics, David C. Young, estimates that a pentathlon victory, which could be paid in a variety of forms (for example, jars of olive oil), was worth more money than a full year's labor.

The last recorded ancient Olympic pentathlon winner was Publius Asklepiades of Corinth, who won in A.D. 241. In A.D.

A well-known symbol of ancient Olympic Games, *The Discus Thrower*

393, Roman Emperor Theodosius I, a Christian, closed all pagan sanctuaries, including Olympia, effectively ending the ancient Olympic Games. The site was abandoned and, over the centuries, buried by earthquakes and other natural causes. It would be more than 15 centuries before another Olympic multi-event winner would be crowned. In the nineteenth century, German archaeological teams excavated the ancient Olympic site. Soon thereafter the Greeks and the Baron Pierre de Coubertin promoted a revival of the Olympic Games.

The Middle Ages and After

The importance of athletics (and therefore multi-event competitions) decreased as Greek and Roman civilization declined. But the ideal of a versatile, all-around athlete was never lost in the 15 centuries in which the world went without Olympic Games.

During the Viking era (approximately A.D. 800-1250) Norsemen had to pass a number of athletic tests, military in nature. Multi-event contests for Vikings included running, wrestling, throwing heavy spears, and even dashing over moving oars. During the Middle Ages, knights periodically tested their skills in tournaments, many of which used a point scoring system. Aspirants had to pass multi-event tests before knighthood. Knights were asked to excel in numerous physical and martial skills.

Treatises on educational reform in the middle of the sixteenth century called for youths to know how to ride in armor, vault on horseback, practice weightlifting, run, wrestle, and jump for distance and height.

By the early seventeenth century, Robert Dover, an aristocratic lawyer, had reinstated the Olympic Games—in England. These annual affairs, the Olympik Games of the Cotswolds, began in 1612 and lasted more than two centuries. Thousands, including William Shakespeare, came to watch the Cotswold Olympiks, which proved so popular that Dover was held in high esteem by his contemporaries, although today he is much less well known than the modern Olympic Games founder Baron de Coubertin.

Unfortunately, for our purposes, the Dover Olympiks contained no multi-event contest. But the idea was not far off. The Renaissance did much to foster the ideal of versatility. And the Enlightenment (with its new ideas about physical education, as well as many other topics) would provide the setting. Advances in technology and economics provided Europeans with free time. In the mid-1700s, in Dessau, in what is today Germany, students competed in a school pentathlon, a combination of the ancient Greek version and knighthood skills. And, in 1792, in Stockholm, Sweden, an "overall" champion was crowned using a three-event contest (running, throwing a large stone, and swimming).

In the late eighteenth century, Guts Muth, author of the first book on physical education, developed a forerunner of modern scoring tables. Weekly his German pupils' performances in running, jumping, and swimming were awarded points. Much of today's decathlon was portrayed by Guts Muth and later nineteenth-century German reformers who began the Turner Movement (gymnastics in unison).

Meanwhile, track and field was staging a comeback in the first half of the nineteenth century, and it would not be long before multi-events joined the movement. Claims that all-around competitions were held in Ireland in the middle of the nineteenth century are unfounded. Another English Olympic revival, the Much Wenlock Games, offered a pentathlon in the late 1860s. The events were high jumping, long jumping, putting a 36-pound stone, running a half-mile, and climbing a 55-foot rope.

Large numbers of Scots, Irish, and Germans emigrated to America during the nineteenth century, and they brought their games with them. The Scottish Caledonian Games, German Turners, and U.S. colleges fostered the return of track and field, which became popular after the Civil War. Many American meets, especially the Caledonian Games, had an "all-around or general" winner, usually the athlete winning the most events or places.

The lineage of the modern-day decathlon is really found here, with the Scots. Their concept was formalized in 1884 when the U.S. designed a national championship All-Around. This evolved into ten events (100-yard run, shot put, high jump, 880-yard walk, hammer throw, pole vault, 120-yard hurdles, 56 pound weight throw, long jump, and one-mile run) contested in a single day, with only 5 minutes rest between events. Winners had to meet minimum marks in each event and were scored on a points-for-place basis until 1893, when the newly formed Amateur Athletic Union (AAU) generated a scoring table to evaluate each performance.

In 1880 an all-around championship was held at the German Gymnastics Championships. It included a stone throw, pole vault, and long jump. By the 1890s several Scandinavian nations were offering a pentathlon, exactly the same as the ancient Greek event.

Multi-Event Competition in the Olympics

When the Olympic Games were renewed in 1896 in Athens, a multi-event contest was overlooked, as it was in Paris four years later. In 1904, the AAU held its All-Around championships on the same track (but months before) the Olympic Games of St. Louis. It has mistakenly been referred to as an "Olympic" event. It was not. Tom Kiely, an Irishman, won easily.

A tenth-year anniversary Olympics was held in Athens in 1906, and organizers, searching for a multi-event contest, conducted the ancient Greek pentathlon, complete with wrestling. Two years later the British, as they have for most of the twentieth century, neglected multi-events at the 1908 London Olympic Games. It was up to the Swedes to include multi-event contests at the 1912 Olympic Games of Stockholm. And they did so with gusto. The Swedish organizers planned a "modern" pentathlon (based on military events), a track-and-field pentathlon (based on the ancient variety, substituting the 1500-meter run for wrestling), and a decathlon, a ten-event contest.

The word decathlon (from the ancient Greek *deka* = ten, *athlos* = contest) was first used in Scandinavia, as Denmark and Sweden both offered "decathlons" in the early years of the twentieth century with different events, order, and tables. In 1911, using today's ten events and sequence, the Swedes conducted the first modern decathlon as a rehearsal for the Stockholm Olympic Games a year later. The decathlon has not changed since. The Göteborg winner in 1911 was Hugo Weislander, who would finish second to Jim Thorpe and would later inherit the world record and Thorpe's medal.

Early Olympic Decathlon Champions

The Scandinavians took to the decathlon like fish to water. In fact, all but one Olympic decathlon medal awarded before World War II was won by decathletes from either the United States or a Scandinavian nation. American achievements were chiefly a result of talented ex-collegians from America's heartland taking up the event once every four years. Scandinavian success was evidence of a multifaceted view of physical education.

The Berlin Olympic Games, scheduled for 1916, were canceled by World War I. In 1920, Norwegian soldier Helge Lövland edged Brutus Hamilton of the University of Missouri by the smallest margin, before or since, in Olympic decathlon history. Hamilton, while coaching at the University of California at Berkeley, became one of America's best-loved and most successful mentors. Four years later, in 113-degree heat on Paris's 500-meter track, Harold Osborn, a former student at the University of Illinois, won the gold medal just days after he won the Olympic high jump title. He remains the only athlete to have won both the decathlon and an individual event.

In 1928 in Amsterdam, a pair of Finns, Paavo Yröjla and Akilles Järvinen, captured the gold and silver medals. Steady Ken Doherty of Detroit, MI, won the bronze. Doherty's track career spanned six decades. Like Hamilton, he became one of America's best-known coaches (Michigan and Pennsylvania). Doherty was also the director of the prestigious Penn Relays and author of popular training books.

A University of Kansas football and basketball star, "Jarring" Jim Bausch, turned back Järvinen at the Los Angeles Olympic Games in 1932. Bausch is still regarded as the greatest athlete in the history of the University of Kansas, quite a feat when one realizes that four-time Olympic discus winner Al Oerter, Olympic 10-kilometer champ Billy Mills, and hoop star Wilt Chamberlain were all Jayhawks. Ironically, had later sets of scoring tables been used in both 1928 and 1932, Järvinen would have had higher totals than either winner. Such is the subjectivity of the scoring tables.

Germans expected their world-record holder, Hans-Heinrich Sievert, to win the Olympic gold medal in Berlin in 1936. But the United States came up with a used-car salesman from Denver named Glenn Morris, a former student at Colorado State who took up the decathlon in 1936 and broke Sievert's record in just his second meet. The great Morris-Sievert Olympic duel never came off because the German came down with a mysterious illness. Morris rebroke his own world record and led a 1-2-3 U.S. sweep, all of which was brilliantly captured by Leni Riefenstahl's superb film, *Olympiad, Festival of Nations*. Morris immediately retired, undefeated in the decathlon, but made nothing of a Hollywood career, appearing with the lead role in but one film, *Tarzan's Revenge*.

World War II robbed several all-around greats of Olympic opportunities. The most notable was Michigan's Big Bill Watson, who would have been the decathlon favorite both in 1940 and 1944.

The Postwar Era

In 1948, when the Olympic Games were held in London, a 17-year-old schoolboy from California turned all the decathlon

Courtesy of Hershey's Track and Field Youth Program

Rafer Johnson won the most dramatic Olympic decathlon, defeating
C.K. Yang in Rome in 1960.

traditions upside down. The decathlon had been looked upon as an event for the experienced, older athlete. Yet here was Bob Mathias, during two miserable days of London fog, turning back the world's best. He was, and still is, the youngest track-and-field champion in Olympic history. And it was only his third decathlon. After the 1948 Games, Mathias enrolled at Stanford, starred as a running back, and broke and rebroke the decathlon world record. At the 1952 Helsinki Games, Mathias became the first decathlete to win a pair of Olympic titles. He won by more than 900 points, the largest margin in Olympic history. Although just 21, Bob retired, undefeated and four-time national champion. He starred in a movie version of his life, *The Bob Mathias Story,* then served several terms in Congress and was director of the United States Olympic Training Center in Colorado Springs, CO.

The Helsinki Games saw an American sweep of all decathlon medals. New Jersey schoolboy Milt Campbell garnered the silver, and Floyd Simmons captured his second bronze. Four years later, Campbell conquered American teammate and world-record holder Rafer Johnson at the 1956 Melbourne Olympic Games. Milt was one of the most versatile athletes of any age. A year later he broke the world record for the 120-yard hurdles, then turned to a professional football career. He was also a national-class judo competitor and All-American swimmer. He is the only athlete to have been inducted into both the National Swimming and National Track and Field halls of fame.

Much like Milt Campbell four years earlier, Rafer Johnson stepped up from silver to gold, winning the decathlon at the 1960 Olympic Games in Rome. But it was not easy. He had to contend with a UCLA teammate, C.K. Yang of Formosa (now Taiwan). For two hot Italian days and nights they put a moratorium on their friendship and battled for ten events at Rome's Estadio Olympico. With only the 1500-meters remaining, Johnson led by 67 points. If Yang could put 10 seconds between himself and Rafer, the gold medal was his. Rafer dogged C.K.'s every step, finished a few meters back, and won by a slim margin.

Italian spectators chanted, "Give them both the gold medal, give them both the gold medal."

A New Decathlon Era

The 1960s saw the decathlon come of age. Not only did American Phil Mulkey and C.K. Yang take turns breaking Rafer Johnson's world record, but the International Amateur Athletic Federation (IAAF), in 1964, introduced new scoring tables making the decathlon a more balanced event. No longer could the decathlon be won by a handful of good events, but it could now be lost with one bad one. Decathletes had to be proficient in every event.

West German coach Friedel Schirmer, who had finished eighth at the 1952 Helsinki decathlon, helped boost the popularity of the decathlon among his fellow Germans. He insisted that the decathlon was not ten unrelated events, but an event in itself. Balance and focus on new tables were the hallmarks of his training methods, and his athletes had great success during the decade. In 1964 in Tokyo, the American decathlon winning streak, which began in 1932, ended. Germans Willi Holdorf and Hans-Joachim Walde won the gold and bronze, sandwiching Estonian Rein Aun. Paul Herman from little Westmont College (CA) was fourth, and all topped Yang.

Four years later, Schirmer's decathletes claimed all the Olympic medals. American Bill Toomey, a Santa Barbara English teacher, had trained with Schirmer in West Germany for a year. Toomey, Walde, and his world-record holder teammate Kurt Bendlin went 1-2-3 at the Mexico City Games of 1968. Toomey's victory stands apart from those of earlier prominent American decathletes. He was considerably older (his 1969 world record came just short of his 31st birthday), and he competed a great deal more. His numerous efforts proved that a well-trained decathlete can compete frequently at a world-class level. Toomey competed in 38 career decathlons, compared to 26 for Mathias, Campbell, and Johnson *combined*.

Courtesy of Chartmasters

Bruce Jenner set a new decathlon world record in 1976
while winning the Olympic gold medal in Montreal.

Toomey's career was even more remarkable when one learns
that, as a youngster, he had severed all the nerves in his right
wrist, losing almost all feeling. He rebuilt the wrist with therapy,
but the hand bothered him throughout his career. In spite of the
adversity, Toomey won 23 major decathlon meets, including five
U.S. national titles (still a record) and the Olympic gold!

Eastern European nations, especially the Soviet Union, Poland, and East Germany, began to emphasize and promote the decathlon in the early 1970s. At the 1972 Munich Games, Toomey watched from the ABC TV platform as a Soviet, the lanky Nikolay Avilov, replaced him as both Olympic champion and world-record holder. Another Soviet, soldier Leonid Litvenyenko, and Ryszard Katus of Poland won the remaining medals. The top American, diminutive Jeff Bennett, lost the bronze medal to Katus (who later defected to the United States) by a mere ten points. Bennett, who attended tiny Oklahoma Christian College, stood but 5 feet, 8 inches, and weighed in at only 152 pounds. But he was a fierce competitor and had the heart of a giant. His battle for the final medal in Munich was the closest in Olympic decathlon annals. An unnoticed but respectable tenth in Munich was a little-known American named Bruce Jenner.

Courtesy of Iris Hensel

Britain's Daley Thompson dominated the 1980s by winning a pair of Olympic gold medals and setting four world records.

The Age of Boycotts

Jenner had set two world decathlon records in the months before the Olympic Games of 1976, and Montreal was to be a showdown with the defending champion, Avilov. From the opening gun it was obvious that Jenner was on a roll, and after the first day, he was just a few points behind German Guido Kratschmer and Avilov. With his best events on the second day, Jenner steamrolled the field. With only the 1500-meters remaining, the question was not whether Jenner would raise his own world record, but by how much. Unlike most decathletes, he looked forward to running the last event.

As Jenner rested on the infield, Litvenyenko tapped him on the shoulder and remarked, "Bruce, you are going to be Olympic champion." "Thanks," Bruce chirped. Litvenyenko gazed at Jenner for a few moments and then asked, "Bruce, are you going to be a millionaire?" Jenner just laughed. In the 1500-meters Jenner ran conservatively at first, then gunned it at the bell, clocking the final 400 meters in an eye-opening 61 seconds. He had recorded a lifetime best in his final event, 4:12.61, and a gaping world record, 8618 points. Someone shoved an American flag in his hand, and his victory lap, on prime-time television, was fabled stuff.

Because the decathlon was an infant event in Africa, the 1976 Games boycott by many African nations left the decathlon medal placings unaffected. The burly and bearded Kratschmer won the silver medal, and Avilov settled for the bronze. Jenner retired without delay, even leaving his vaulting poles in the Montreal stadium tunnel. For him there would be new worlds to conquer. But he did recall that one athlete, who had finished 18th, a British teenager named Daley Thompson, had asked a lot of questions.

Another boycott reared its ugly head in 1980, this one led by U.S. President Jimmy Carter. American and German track-and-field contingents did not participate in the Moscow Olympic Games, robbing the decathlon field of both Bob Coffman, a raw Texan who was the Pan American champion, and the new world-record holder, Guido Kratschmer. But the British team did travel to the Soviet Union, and Daley Thompson was not seriously challenged. With 20-20 hindsight, it is difficult to see how either the American or the German could have coped with Thompson in Moscow. Daley began his 1980s reign, now labeled "the Daley decade."

Thompson won the European crown in 1982 in Athens with a new world record, then captured the IAAF's initial World Championship in Helsinki in 1983. In both cases he vanquished giant Jürgen Hingsen, called the "German Hercules." The Thompson/Hingsen matches of the 1980s were classics. The pair broke and rebroke the world record on seven occasions, but head-to-head the Brit never lost.

In 1984, when the Summer Olympic Games returned to the United States for the first time in 52 years, it was the Eastern Bloc nations, led by the Soviets, who stayed at home. No matter in the decathlon, since Thompson was once again supreme. Daley, like Bob Mathias before him, won a second gold medal, again broke the world record, and again made Hingsen settle for the silver. West German Siggi Wentz won the bronze, and it is difficult to envision any Eastern Bloc decathletes who could have broken up the top three. Two years later at the 1986 European Championships in Stuttgart, West Germany, the Thompson-Hingsen-Wentz trio again went 1-2-3 in what many still consider to be the best international decathlon ever.

In 1987 an injury slowed Daley at the second World Championships in Rome. Now 29, he competed anyway and finished ninth, his first defeat in nine seasons. Hingsen, suffering broken ribs, did not finish. In their absence, East Germany's Torsten Voss, a 24-year-old mechanic, held off Wentz for the win.

At the Seoul Olympic Games of 1988, favorite Siggi Wentz was injured and could not compete. Thompson, in his fourth Olympics, was also injured and short on conditioning. But like a true gladiator with a competitive zest, he went to the arena.

There he watched a 6' 6" East German medical student, Christian Schenk, use a 7' 5" high jump to propel him to the gold medal. Voss was second, and Canadian Dave Steen, a Cal-Berkeley student, edged Thompson for the bronze medal.

The 1980s had seen a terrific run by Thompson, 12 consecutive wins, all in major meets. And he did it against top competition. The decade witnessed an explosion in the number of world-class decathletes. A score of more than 8000 points, once almost unheard of, was bettered over 500 times in the 1980s, with the Soviets and Germans (West and East) far ahead of the remainder of the world. For Americans it was the worst decade yet. For the first eight years of the 1980s Americans could scarcely be found in the annual world rankings.

Enter Dan and Dave

After the 1988 Seoul Olympic Games, American decathlon fortunes abruptly reversed course. Californian Dave Johnson led the resurgence, and his score for 1989 topped the world list. In 1990, Visa, U.S.A., the credit card giant, initiated a national program to help return U.S. decathlon fortunes to their former prominence. Later that year, Johnson and Dan O'Brien, a former University of Idaho star, swept the Goodwill Games decathlon in Seattle, WA. Again Johnson's best score led the world list. A year later it was O'Brien who threatened Daley Thompson's world record and who captured the third World Championship crown in Tokyo. In decathlon circles, thanks to Visa, the United States was back.

In 1992, shoe giant Reebok featured both O'Brien and Johnson in a multimillion-dollar advertising campaign entitled "Dan or Dave? To Be Settled in Barcelona." The campaign raised decathlon popularity in the United States, but neither O'Brien nor Johnson was fortunate enough to win at the 1992 Barcelona Olympic Games. O'Brien, suffering a stress fracture, was unable to clear a pole vault bar at the U.S. Olympic Trials and did not make the

American team. Johnson won the Trials but suffered a broken bone in his foot just weeks before the Games. He kept the injury secret, competed with a heart of gold, and limped home with the bronze medal. Czechoslovakia's Robert Zmelik won in Barcelona, and Spain's Antonio Peñalver was second. One month later, O'Brien met Zmelik at DecaStar, an invitational decathlon in Talence, France. Not only did the American win by more than 500 points, but he broke Daley Thompson's eight-year-old world record, running up 8891 points.

A year later, O'Brien captured another world title, this time in Stuttgart, Germany, where his major foes were Eduard Hämäläinen of Belarus and Germany's tall Paul Meier. In 1994, Hämäläinen had the world's top score, 8735 points, while O'Brien went undefeated with three efforts over 8700. A year later it was O'Brien with a hat trick, winning a third IAAF World Championship, and once again Hämäläinen was his main nemesis.

Courtesy of Victah Sailer

Dave Johnson

Courtesy of Iris Hensel

Dan O'Brien

At the 1996 Atlanta Olympic Games, Dan O'Brien reigned supreme, finally winning the elusive gold medal. Behind him were young German Frank Busemann, Czech soldier Tomas Dvorak, American Steve Fritz, and Hämäläinen. A year later Dvorak won the IAAF world title in Athens, and again, American Steve Fritz was fourth. O'Brien made a brief comeback in 1998 to capture the Goodwill Games. And in 1999 (on July 4th no less) Dvorak finally exceeded O'Brien's world record with a gaudy 8994 score, finishing just shy of the magic 9000 point barrier.

Fritz, Chris Huffins, and Tom Pappas have been the American champions since the O'Brien era. In 2000 Pappas, Huffins, and veteran Kip Janvrin made the U.S. Olympic team.

2

Meet the
U.S. Decathletes

HUFFINS, CHRIS

Height: 6' 2"

Weight: 190 lb

Born: April 15, 1970

Hometown: Brooklyn, NY

Career Highlights: 1998, 1999 U.S. Champion; 1999 World Championships bronze medalist; 1999 Pan Am Games gold medalist; holds decathlon WR in 100m (10.22). 2000 Olympic team member; 2nd at 2000 Olympic Trials.

Huffins was first intrigued by the decathlon in 1991 when he sat in the stands with a broken toe, watching the Cal decathletes work out. He bragged to his coach, Ed Miller, "I can do that." He has made good on that braggadoccio. And the timing couldn't be better. He's coming off his best year, winning the 1999 U.S. Outdoor and Pan Am titles and taking the bronze at the World Championships.

2000: Battling an upset stomach, placed 2nd in Olympic Trials (8285).

1999: Won USA Outdoors (8350)... won gold at Pan Am Games... bronze at World Champs (8547)... best of 8547.

1998: Won USA Outdoors (8694 PR)...won DecaJam (8315)...did not finish Gotzis...2nd at Goodwill Games (8576)...did not finish Talence...ranked #5 in world (#2 U.S.) by T&FN... best of 8694.

1997: 2nd in USA Outdoors (8458)...did not finish World Champs...won Talence (8425)...ranked #7 in world (#2 U.S.) by T&FN...best of 8458.

1996: 3rd in Olympic Trials (8546); included decathlon WR 10.22 in 100...10th in Olympic Games (8300)...ranked #10 in world (#3 U.S.) by T&FN... best of 8546.

1995: 2nd at USA Outdoors (8351 PR)...8th at World Champs (8193)...ranked #8 in world (#2 U.S.) by T&FN... best of 8351.

1994: Did not compete.

1993: Won NCAA (8007 PR)...9th in USA Outdoors (7726)...won Pac-10 (7671)... PR of 26-3.5 in LJ...ranked #9 U.S. by T&FN... best of 8007.

1992: 15th in Olympic Trials (7662w)... best of 7854.

1991: Won TJ at Pac-10; 3rd in LJ...12th in LJ at NCAAs; 13th in TJ qualifying...tied for 19th in LJ qualifying at USA Outdoors... best of 26-1.5 (LJ).

1990: 8th in 100 heat at NCAAs...7th in 100 semi at USA Outdoors... best of 25-2.5 (LJ).

1989: 16th in NCAA Indoor LJ...12th in LJ at NCAAs...23rd in LJ qualifying at USA Champs...2nd in LJ, 8th in TJ; 5th in 100 heat at USA Juniors... best of 25-10 (LJ).

1988: Best of 23-6.5 (LJ).

JANVRIN, KIP

Height: 6' 0"

Weight: 185 lb

Born: July 8, 1965

Hometown: Guthrie Center, IA

School: University of Tennessee

Jarvin's longevity is unprecedented in U.S. decathlon history. He has been nationally-ranked since 1989 and he has completed 69 of 71 decathlons. He has 60 scores over 7000 points, and when he scored 8029 points in the USA-German dual meet in August 2000, it was his 24th meet over 8000 points, again the best ever by an American.

2000: Placed 3rd at Olympic Trials (8057 points)...won USA-German meet with 8029 points.

1999: Placed 4th at USA Champs...ranked #5 in U.S. by T&FN...best of 8017.

1998: Placed 4th at USA Champs...ranked #5 in U.S. by T&FN...best of 8081.

1997: Placed 4th at USA Champs...ranked #4 in U.S. by T&FN...best of 8228.

1996: Placed 4th at Olympic Trials...ranked #4 in U.S. by T&FN...best of 8462 (windy).

1995: Placed 7th at USA Champs...Pan American Games champion...ranked #5 in U.S. by T&FN ...best of 8057.

1994: Placed 3rd at USA Champs...ranked #10 in world (#3 U.S.) by T&FN...best of 8287.

1993: Placed 4th at USA Champs...ranked #5 in U.S. by T&FN...best of 8052.

1992: Placed 8th at Olympic Trials...ranked #10 in U.S. by T&FN...best of 7949.

1991: Placed 11th at USA Champs...best of 7943.

1990: Placed 6th at USA Champs...ranked #5 in U.S. by T&FN...best of 8113 (windy).

1989: Placed 4th at USA Champs...ranked #4 in U.S. by T&FN...best of 9994.

1988: Placed 8th at NCAA Champs...best of 7482.

1987: Placed 11th at NCAA Champs...best of 7545.

1986: Best of 7323.

PAPPAS, TOM

Height: 6' 5"

Weight: 204 lb

Born: September 6, 1976

Hometown: Azalea, OR

Pappas participated in football, baseball, wrestling, and basketball in high school, where he was Junior class president. Pappas's grandfather was a professional wrestler who encouraged him to try the sport as well. His father, Nick, constructed a full-size wrestling ring in their basement so Tom and his two brothers could take turns body slamming each other. Pappas's competitive nature comes directly from his father, who has dealt with paralysis most of his life after becoming a victim of polio before age two. Despite being physically challenged, Nick Pappas became the family's first world-record holder when he and a partner claimed a land speed record at the Bonneville Salt Flats in a vehicle that achieved a top velocity of more than 700 kilometers per hour. In

1995, Tom Pappas began training as a decathlete, winning his first-ever decathlon with 6746 points. In 1998, Pappas was named to the GTE Academic All-America District IV second team with a 3.83 grade-point-average in recreation and leisure.

2000: Won Olympic trials decathlon with a PR 8467 points.

1999: Won NCAA Outdoors...set PR and collegiate record 8463 at Tempe, AZ, on March 19; 2nd at USA Outdoors (8187)...dnf World Champs (5895, no height in pole vault)...best of 8463.

1998: Did not compete due to knee injury.

1997: Won SEC Champs...8th at NCAA Outdoors...best of 7677.

1996: Best of 7499.

1995: Won USA Juniors...won Pan Am Juniors...best of 7198.

3

The Nature of the Decathlon

The decathlon is an athletic competition containing ten different track-and-field (athletics) contests and won by the participant amassing the highest total score. It is an Olympic multi-event sport for men. The women's counterpart is a seven-event contest called "heptathlon." Virtually all that we offer here about the decathlon can also be applied to the women's heptathlon. As we saw in the previous chapter the decathlon has its ancestry in the ancient Greek Games and reveals the Greek model of a balanced, all-around athlete.

What the Decathlon Requires

The decathlon is a two-day miniature track meet designed to ascertain the sport's best all-around athlete. Within its competitive rules, each athlete must sprint for 100 meters, long jump, heave a 16-pound ball, high jump, and run 400 meters, all in that very order, on the first day. On the second day the athlete runs a 110-meter hurdle race over 42-inch barriers, hurls the discus, pole vaults, tosses a javelin, and at the end of the contest, races 1500 meters, virtually a mile.

All-around contests abound. Many individual sports from gymnastics to rodeo to Nordic skiing to equestrian have all-around contests designed to measure versatility within that sport. But since track and field (athletics) is the most fundamental (some say the first or basic) sport, where its participants run, jump, and throw, its all-around test, the decathlon, measures those elementary athletic talents. Speed, strength, agility, spring, and endurance are embodied within its measurable objectives. While one athlete may be faster, another stronger, and yet a third a better jumper, the decathlon attempts to determine who, among the three, is the best all-around or general athlete.

The skills of the decathlete are not specific to any sport. Although all sporting contests need fast, strong, and agile athletes, they also demand specific skills. Those skills, (*e.g.*, making a 20-foot jump shot, hitting a curveball, or kicking a field goal) are difficult to master, specific to each sport, but not general in nature. This is why there can be no doubt that decathlon champions are the best all-around athletes in the world. Making a case that decathletes are the "world's best athletes" is harder since some athletes with honed *specific* talents, such as Michael Jordan or Tiger Woods, may be so proficient in their unique skills as to overshadow a decathlete with terrific general competency.

The decathlete does not have to be exceptional in any one event to be the champion in the ten events. He must range from being at least adequate in his weak events to being outstanding in his stronger events. Because he must do well in three running, one hurdling, three jumping, and three throwing events, he has inadequate chance to perfect and polish any one of the events. So he must compromise. And therein lies the nature of the decathlon. It is a compromise that demands concessions in preparation so as to maximize the total score. In his training the decathlete must strive to improve his technique, gain strength without sacrificing speed or spring and vice versa, and acquire the endurance that will escort him through a competition which, in many cases, lasts 8-10 hours each day.

An international scoring table is provided to evaluate and award points for each performance. The winner is the athlete who has the most points after ten events. So the decathlon is the only event in which it doesn't really matter if the athlete finishes first, third, or worse in a particular event. The score is the thing, and the decathlete competes against a scoring table, and in reality, against his own ability and standards. A score of 8000 points (averaging 800 points per event) is a rule-of-thumb cutoff for a world-class decathlete. Few major international meetings will ever be won with a score of less than 8000 points. There is some subjectivity within the scoring tables. More on this later.

Courtesy of Victah Sailer

Mental factors play an important role: Decathletes must stay focused for two days of competition.

Mental factors play a greater role than they do in other events. Many coaches talk of a "decathlon mentality," meaning the athlete's ability to stay focused throughout the ten events, to get psyched up for each attempt or race, and to shrug off disappointment and get on with the next trial. In the decathlon there are chances to recuperate from mistakes.

Decathletes also differ from most athletes in their reaction to a completed meet. Ask a decathlete to assess his recently completed performance and he is seldom satisfied. Rarely does a decathlete achieve a personal-record (PR) performance in every event. No matter how well one does, whether he wins or sets a record, the decathlete can always find room for improvement. There is always a "wait until next time" attitude.

Additionally the decathlon is the most neighborly of all track events. Because the same athletes are together for the better part of two days, and the rules require a minimum of 30 minutes rest between events, there is much time to chat on the field. And much of the time is used in helping one another, appraising technique, verifying takeoff points, giving advice and reassurance, even using others' equipment.

In the decathlon the opponent is rarely another athlete. The struggle is against time, distance, fatigue, one's inner fear of weakness or failure, and the scoring tables. The opponent is oneself. Other decathletes are comrades, friends who help others do their best. Rarely are they hostile. Every decathlete concentrates on doing his utmost without attempting to diminish the efforts of others.

Decathletes Come in All Shapes and Sizes

Unlike wrestling or boxing, there are no weight classes in the decathlon. Its combatants come in varied shapes and sizes. World class competitors have been as small as Jeff Bennett who was 5' 8" and weighed just under 150 pounds when he first broke 8000 points back in 1970, or as tall as Rick Wanamaker, a 6' 8", 210-pound center on the Drake University basketball team. Bennett was an Olympic competitor while Wanamaker was the first National Collegiate Athletic Association decathlon champion. Few have been heavier than Rudy Ziegert's 235 pounds or Russ Hodge's 225. The former, a Russian soldier, scored over 8000 points on numerous occasions. Hodge held the world record in 1966.

Here is a range of heights and weights for most world-class competitors:

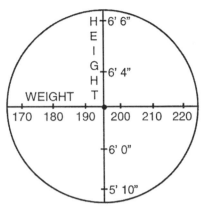

Average size: 6' 2", 195 lb

Since decathletes score over a wide range of points on the scoring tables, there is a wide range of shapes, sizes, and body types. But as one gets closer to world-class level the sizes get remarkably similar, averaging about 6' 0" to 6' 3" in height and 180 to 200 pounds. This may be an "ideal" size. But many decathletes with prototypical deviations from the ideal size (small and wiry, tall and rangy, short and bulky, tall and bulky) have all been successful and do not fit the ideal description.

Here is a range of heights and weights for decathletes from the novice to national-class range.

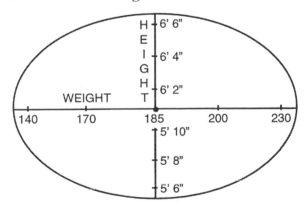

Average size: 6' 0", 185 lb

Like training, height and weight are a decathlete's compromise. Athletes who are tall have a leverage advantage in the throwing events and a high center of gravity for the hurdles and high jump. On the other side of the ledger, tall athletes have a more difficult time unwinding from starting blocks and staying within the throwing rings.

Heavier athletes obviously have more bulk to push the weights. But for running and jumping events they must carry and lift that bulk. The pole vault and 1500-meter run are particularly difficult for heavier athletes. Youngsters should not be concerned with height and weight. Nature will take care of that.

One game some decathlon fans play around with is to assign points on a per pound basis. Just divide the decathlete's best score by his weight. Anything over 45 points per pound is exceptional. The results may be interesting, but the exercise is just for fun. The conclusion is obvious. Although many coaches look for an ideal size decathlete, any size will do. Decathletes come in all shapes and sizes.

A Quick Look at Some of the Events

Here is some basic information about each of the ten decathlon events.

100 Meters

This event measures basic leg speed. Each race/heat will have between three and eight runners. You will push off a set of starting blocks at the start as a reaction to a starter's pistol, sprint for 100 meters, and lean at the finish line. The race can be timed with a handheld stopwatch to the tenth of a second, or by an automatic timing device, which will catch the runners in 1/100ths of a second.

Long Jump

The athlete runs toward the landing area, plants his takeoff foot on an 8-inch "toeboard" (named for obvious reasons), and leaps into a sand-filled pit. The distance is measured from the mark made in the pit that is closest to the takeoff board. Speed and accuracy are secondary to leaping ability. Each athlete has only three chances, and only the best jump counts in the scoring.

Shot Put

The shot put measures basic arm strength. Again, each athlete has three tries, counting only the best effort for scoring. The athlete attempts to push or "put" (not throw) a 16-pound iron ball so that it lands within a sector of 40 degrees. The throwing circle is 7 feet wide and made of concrete. Efforts do not count if the athlete oversteps the throwing circle or if the shot lands outside of the sector lines.

High Jump

The high jump is another explosive event in which the athlete must approach the bar and landing area, gather himself, and leap (always off one foot) over a crossbar. The landing pit is usually made of foam rubber. The crossbar is raised, usually by 3 centimeters, and an athlete is eliminated after three consecutive misses. The highest height cleared is used for scoring.

400 Meters

A century ago a quarter-mile (440-yard) race was deemed an endurance test. Today its metric equivalent is almost an all-out sprint. The athlete runs the entire distance in lanes, and as in the 100-meter race, may have anywhere from two to three competitors. The 400 meters tests both speed and stamina and ends the first day's competition.

110-Meter Hurdles

The initial event of the second day combines speed and agility. The athletes must sprint (not jump) over a series of ten barriers, 42 inches high (39 inches at the high school level), which are placed 10 yards apart. The athlete must both sprint and stretch his stride pattern so as to take only three steps between hurdles. Hurdles may not be deliberately knocked down.

Discus Throw

The discus, which weighs 2 kilograms and is about 8 inches in diameter, has aerodynamic qualities. Again, only three tries are allowed, and the athlete, while turning one time, must stay within an 8' 2" concrete circle. The discus must land within a 40-degree sector. Only the best throw counts in the scoring.

Pole Vault

Technically this is the decathlon's most difficult event. While grasping the upper end of a 14- to 15-foot fiberglass vaulting pole, the athlete races toward the pit, plants the pole in a takeoff box, and swings himself up and over a crossbar, eventually landing in a foam rubber pit. Sound easy? It takes lots of practice.

Javelin

The javelin is a metal spear approximately 8 feet in length and weighing 800 grams (just under 2 pounds). At all levels except high school, the javelin must land point first within the sector, which is 29 degrees wide. Each athlete is given three attempts, and the best throw is scored.

1500 Meters

The final test is one of endurance, 3 3/4 laps around the 400-meter track. Rarely does the decathlete have the luxury of loafing during this event. He must give his best effort since—at approximately 6 points for every second—places, scores, and records (personal or otherwise) will be at stake.

What Are the Decathlon Rules?

Every decathlete should be familiar with track-and-field rules. With a few exceptions, the decathlon events are conducted by the same rules as the individual events. The exceptions can be found in the decathlon/multi-event section of rule books. Unfortunately, in the United States there are four different rule books being used, depending on the level of competition.

- International meets   IAAF Rule Book

- National/domestic meets   USA T&F Rule Book

- Collegiate meets   NCAA Rule Book

- High school meets   National High School Rule Book

Just make certain under which set of rules your decathlon meet is being conducted. But don't despair. The differences in the rules are very minor. See Chapter 13, "Olympic and Decathlon Organizations," for information about where to obtain various rule books.

Here are a few of the differences between normal track-and-field rules and decathlon practices.

1. The decathlon must always be held on two consecutive days and contested in the following order:

First Day	Second Day
100-Meter Dash	110-Meter Hurdles
Long Jump	Discus Throw
Shot Put	Pole Vault
High Jump	Javelin Throw
400-Meter Dash	1500-Meter Run

The rule books will also list the order for other multi-event competitions including men's pentathlon, women's heptathlon, and indoor multi-events.

2. An interval of at least 30 minutes should be allowed between the time one event ends and the next event begins. At the discretion of the games committee, this interval can be altered.

3. Each competitor will be allowed only three attempts in the long jump, shot put, discus throw, and javelin throw.

4. It is recommended that fully automatic timing be used. If the meet is manually timed, each competitor shall be timed by three timekeepers independently. If the times differ, the median time shall be adopted. If for any reason only two register times, and they differ, the slower of the two shall be adopted as official.

5. In running events the competition will be disqualified after three false starts (two in NCAA).

6. In the high jump and pole vault, the games committee will set the starting heights, and the bar will be raised by 3 centimeters (for high jump) and 10 cm (for pole vault).

7. All measurements are metric. It is recommended that all measurements be made with a steel tape. Discus and javelin throws are measured to the least *even* centimeter. In the shot put, throws are measured to the least centimeter.

8. Section and lane assignments for running events are determined by lot. No fewer than three competitors shall start in any section. In the final event, the 1500 meters, the leaders should run in the same heat. If athletes are grouped, the referee shall have the power to rearrange the groups.

9. Hurdles are run in adjacent lanes, except in collegiate meets where hurdles are placed in alternate lanes.

10. If a competitor fouls another competitor in any event, he shall lose the points gained for that event but shall be allowed to compete in succeeding events unless the referee deems that the loss of points is not a sufficient penalty.

11. Athletes must make an attempt at each event. This rule is designed to guarantee that the athlete intends to do a full decathlon and not just set records or get a workout in single events. Athletes failing to start any event are considered to have abandoned the competition. They receive no final score and are not included in the final placing.

12. The event scores, cumulative scores, and places shall be announced to the competitors at the completion of each event.

13. The winner of the competition is the athlete who has scored the highest number of points on the IAAF scoring tables (which conveniently are included in the NCAA Rule Book). If there is a tie score, the athlete scoring the higher number of points in the most events shall be awarded the higher place. If a tie still remains, then the competitor who has earned the highest number of points in any single event will be given the higher place. If the tie still exists, then the second highest number of points is used, and so on. This rule applies to all decathlon competitions except those governed by NCAA rules. The NCAA does not break ties.

4

Let's Get Started

Unlike pet supplies or health foods, the decathlon is not found in the phone book. If you want to try the decathlon, who do you call? Where do you go?

Future multi-eventers are most likely already members of a track team, perhaps a community club or a high school or college team. They already have some experience with some events and an interest in others. With but a vague notion about what the decathlon really is, they may be introduced to it by a coach who senses that the athlete has some talent to meet the demands of multi-events. If this is your introduction to the decathlon, consider yourself fortunate. The advantages of being introduced to the decathlon this way are numerous: a track and equipment provided by the club or school, an interested mentor to enter you in meets, and perhaps others to train with.

Of course it is not always that easy. Often "decathlon talent" is not easily observable, or coaches may be too busy or simply uninterested. School facilities/equipment may be unavailable.

Rarely are school authorities or coaches hostile, and you are unlikely to have the experience former NCAA decathlon champ Ed Miller had while preparing for the 1976 U. S. Olympic Trials.

With the meet but a few weeks off, he was arrested for hopping a fence at a local college track to work out. Dissatisfied with his explanation, authorities handcuffed, fingerprinted, and booked him. You probably won't have to go that far in defense of your devotion to the decathlon, but you should admire Miller's commitment. Miller has since become one of America's top decathlon coaches.

Courtesy of the Dan O'Brien Youth Foundation

Age-group multi-events abound, providing young athletes the opportunity to develop good technique early in their careers.

If your coach, parents, or friends don't introduce the decathlon to you, then introduce it to them. If you are a member of the local track team, ask the coach for advice in preparing for the decathlon. If you are not part of a track and field program, contact the local coach, a parent, or a former decathlete. Don't be a pest, but ask your contacts if they will take some time to help you with a few events. Don't ask if they will be willing to coach you full-time. No one has that sort of time available. Just ask if they would be willing to observe you doing a few events. Make sure that it fits into their schedule.

If you are dealing with the local school coach, suggest convenient times, like before or after formal practice sessions. School coaches may allow you the use of equipment, such as shots, discs, vaulting poles, or hurdles. They have the keys to the equipment shed. Be polite and solicit information, perhaps names of other local decathletes. Some college athletes may be home for the summer. Some veteran athletes may be training nearby. All will know the names and sites of a few meets, and some may even have an entry blank.

Many athletes don't know what a decathlon is until they are in one. Enter a meet. Go and compete, even if you have not prepared for some of the events. You'll meet other novices. You'll network. You'll get an idea about your own level of competency and how much training is necessary for success. You'll talk about the next meet. You'll be hooked.

In the past 25 years I have had literally thousands of calls about the decathlon from athletes, parents, and even coaches. The most commonly asked questions, especially from novices, are:

- How do I find out about decathlon competitions?
- What meets are available/open to me?
- How should I go about training for the decathlon?
- How do I find a coach?
- Where can I obtain a set of scoring tables?

This chapter attempts to answer questions concerning the availability of decathlon meets in a systematic fashion. The remaining questions are dealt with later in the text.

Availability of Meets

As recently as 1967 there were fewer than ten decathlons held annually in the entire United States. Today the list exceeds 300. There are a number of reasons for the growing popularity. First, back in 1970 the NCAA, following the lead of the National Association of Intercollegiate Athletics (NAIA), made the decathlon a scoring event in its national championships. College conferences, starting with the IC4A, followed suit. For the first time, college coaches began to recruit and train young men as decathletes and not as specialists. The popularity of the event mushroomed. Second, Bill Toomey's career showed that decathletes, if properly trained, could do more than one or two meets a season. Third, decathlon interest picked up with the entrance of Visa, U.S.A. as an event sponsor and Reebok's 1992 ad campaign that featured two world-class decathletes, Dave Johnson and Dan O'Brien.

Now decathlon meets abound. You just need to know where to look. Today U.S. decathlon/multi-event opportunities are available by:

- Age
- Region
- Educational level
- Ability
- Disability

While there is some overlap, this is a convenient way to explain where the meets are.

Age

At the younger ages, there are several national programs for teenagers and subteen decathletes.

Youth Athletics Program

In recent years, the national governing body for track and field, USA T&F has formalized a program for youngsters. The organization sponsors a national championship meet and maintains national records for three categories. Although no decathlon is offered, abbreviated versions of multi-event competitions are provided to athletes even under ten years of age:

    I. **Bantam** (10 years and under) Triathlon

        (high jump - 6 lb shot put - 200m)

    II. **Midget** (11-12) Pentathlon

        (80m hurdles-high jump-6 lb shot put-long jump-800m)

    III. **Youth** (13-14) Pentathlon

        (100m hurdles-long jump-4kg shotput-high jump-800m)

For additional information about the Youth Athletics program, contact the chair of the Youth Athletics Committee of USA T&F:

Kim L. Haines   Home: 406-677-2427
P.O. Box 416   Office: 406-677-2224
Seeley Lake, MT 59868 Fax: 406-677-2949

Junior Olympic Program

Since 1981 the National Junior Olympic program features decathlon competition at national championships each July for:

    I. **Intermediate Boys** (15-16)
       Here the events and scoring tables are standard, but lighter implements and lower hurdles are used.

II. **Young Men** (17-18)
   Again, lighter implements and lower hurdles.

Each year approximately 25-30 athletes compete in each division. Entry standards vary.

The nation is divided into Junior Olympic regions, and most regions (many are simply states) offer a regional qualifying meet, usually in June. If you do not know your regional Junior Olympic (JO) representative, simply contact the name of the individual above (Youth Athletics). The USA T&F Press Information Office (or web site: usatf.org) will know, by January 1 of each year, the dates, sites, and names of meet directors for the national Youth Athletics and National Junior Olympic championship meets. Address:

USA Track and Field
One RCA Dome, Suite 140   Tel: (317) 261-0500
Indianapolis, IN 46225   Web site: www.usatf.org

AAU Junior Olympics Program

There is a corollary nationwide program, simply called AAU Junior Olympics, which mirrors the USA T&F Youth/Junior Olympics program. In a sense both groups run similar programs. The AAU deals with many other sports, while USA T&F deals only with track and field. The age groups and multi-events for both Junior Olympics programs are the same:

Division	Age	Event
Bantam	10 and under	Triathlon
Midget	11-12	Pentathlon
Youth	13-14	Pentathlon
Intermediate	15-16	Decathlon
Young Men	17-18	Decathlon

There are 58 AAU associations, and many offer meets at the association level. Athletes advance to regional meets and, in late July of each year, compete at a national AAU Junior Olympics competition. It is estimated that approximately 200-250 young men compete in AAU JO multis annually.

The national track-and field-director of AAU Junior Olympics is Don Kavades:

Don Kavades	Tel: 209-784-5485
P.O. Box 1433	Fax: 209-781-4535
283 N. South Street	E-mail: dkavadas@ocsnet.net
Porterville, CA 93250	

National USA T&F Junior Program

Until 1972 the AAU Junior Championships were open to those who, regardless of age, had not won a national (AAU) championship, foreign championship, or collegiate (NCAA, NAIA, IC4A) title. Pan American and Olympic team members were also ineligible. The first U.S. junior championships were conducted in 1900, and the definition held until 1972. Today the United States uses the standard international definition of a "junior"; that is, athletes must be at least 14 and cannot reach age 20 in the year of competition.

Each year USA T&F conducts a National Junior Championship meet, usually in the third week of June. There are no regional junior meets. Rather, athletes qualify for this meet by meeting a standard sometime during the spring season. Decathletes (who may either be college freshman or high school athletes as long as they do not turn 20 that year) must meet a minimum qualifying score. In recent years they could meet the standard by scoring 6000 points with high school implements/hurdles or 5950 points using the international (college) implements. Each year the standards are adjusted slightly. Approximately 10-20 decathletes compete annually.

Every even-numbered year (1996-1998-2000) the top two finishers qualify to represent the United States at the World Junior Championships. Every odd-numbered year (1995-1997-1999) the top two finishers represent the United States at the Pan-American Junior Championships. In recent years additional international competition has been provided to the top junior decathletes.

Masters (Veterans) Programs

Recently the United States has witnessed a proliferation of masters or veteran programs. A masters competitor must be 40 years of age (there is a sub-masters level beginning at age 35). Veterans compete in age groups of five years (*e.g.* 40-44, 45-49, 50-54, etc.), and today there are decathletes over the age of 90 still competing.

Each season USA T&F conducts a National Masters T&F Championship, which includes a decathlon. In addition, national indoor and outdoor pentathlon meets are offered.

The governing body for veterans affairs is the World Association of Veteran Athletes (WAVA). It sponsors the World Veterans Championships every odd-numbered year. These are popular affairs. In 1989 the world meet was conducted in Eugene, OR, and drew 123 decathletes.

In addition, there are a number of regional veterans meets, the most popular being held in Lincoln, NE, and Neosho, MO, each summer and in Thomasville, NC, each fall.

As the age groups advance, shorter hurdles (*e.g.* 39 inches at age 40, 36 inches at age 50, etc) and lighter implements are used.

For scoring the decathlon WAVA adopted age-graded tables in 1989. These tables incorporate a series of age factors and age standards that take into consideration how much athletic performances decline as someone ages. The factors compare performances over the years and, when applied to the IAAF decathlon scoring tables, offer a more meaningful score. They can be obtained from a very helpful monthly newspaper entitled

National Masters News (NMN), which is indispensable for veteran athletes since it contains meet schedules and results.

National Masters News

Subscription Dept.   Tel: 818-577-7233
P.O. Box 5185   Web site: www.nationalmastersnews.com
Pasadena, CA 91107   E-mail: suzy@nationalmastersnews.com

One decathlete you'll get to meet if you decide to take up the veterans decathlon challenge is Rex Harvey, an engineer and former Air Force officer. Harvey began competing in 1965 and has completed so many decathlons that he'll soon be the first athlete in history to amass more than a million career points. He has been the WAVA world champ on several occasions and is always active on U.S. and WAVA multiple-event committees. Barbara Kousky, chairperson of USA T&F Masters Track, will also be helpful.

Rex Harvey   Barbara Kousky
160 Chatham Way   5319 Donald Street
Mayfield Heights, OH 44124   Eugene, OR 97405-4820
Tel: 216-446-0559   Tel: 503-687-8787
                                Office: 503-687-1989
                                Fax: 503-687-1016

Finally, for the numerically conscious, *National Masters News* and *Track & Field News* both have "Masters Age Records" available. It is an annual booklet which lists men's and women's world and U.S. age bests for all track, and, field events, age 35 and up.

Region

For track-and-field purposes, the nation is sliced up a number of ways: by USA T&F association, by state, and by region of the country.

State Associations

USA T&F has divided the nation by association districts, most of which conduct outdoor track-and-field championships. For example, the Potomac Valley Association of USA T&F conducts track and field in the Washington, DC,-Maryland-northern Virginia area. Some of the associations conduct a decathlon with their annual meet, some conduct it separately, and some ignore the multi-events. Currently about a dozen of the associations annually offer a decathlon.

Contact your local association for a schedule of meets. If you are unaware of who the association director is, you can log on to www.usatf.org and click on "associations." This link will supply you with a list of all the associations and the names, addresses and phone numbers of all directors.

State Games

In the 1980s a wave of mini-Olympic affairs, conducted on a regional basis, swept the nation. Encouraged by the success of the Florida Sunshine State Games, the New York Empire State Games, and Pennsylvania's Keystone State Games, 35 states now offer athletic contests, usually over a one-week period in midsummer. All offer track and field and about one-half of these have decathlons. Some, like New York, even have regional qualifying meets with decathlons. These are terrific developmental meets for college and high school athletes, who are constantly looking for summer meets.

State Games are normally conducted on the campus of a large college or university. You'll need to contact your state government (many of these athletics contests are run out of the governor's office) to find if a decathlon is offered.

As of early 1999 the following states conducted summer Games:

Alabama	Alabama Sports Festival	late June
Alaska	Greatland Games	late August

Arizona	Grand Canyon Games	late June
California	California State Games	mid-August
Colorado	Colorado Sports Council	late June
Connecticut	Nutmeg Games	late July
D.C.	Capital Games	late June
Florida	Sunshine State Games	early July
Georgia	Georgia State Games	late July
Idaho	First Security Games	early July
Illinois	Prairie State Games	mid-July
Iowa	Iowa Games	early August
Indiana	White River Park State Games	mid-July
Kansas	Sunflower State Games	late July
Kentucky	Bluegrass State Games	late July
Massachusetts	Bay State Games	mid-July
Minnesota	Star of North State Games	late June
Mississippi	State Games of Mississippi	early July
Missouri	Show-Me State Games	late July
Montana	Big Sky State Games	mid-July
Nebraska	Cornhusker State Games	mid-July
New Jersey	Garden State Games	early July
New Mexico	New Mexico State Games	early June
New York	Empire State Games	early August
North Carolina	State Games of North Carolina	late June
North Dakota	Prairie Rose State Games	late July
Ohio	Ohio Games	mid-July
Oklahoma	Sooner State Games	mid-June

Oregon	State Games of Oregon	early July
Pennsylvania	Keystone State Games	early August
Tennessee	Tennessee Sportfest	late June
Texas	Games of Texas	late July
Utah	Utah Summer Games	mid-June
Virginia	Commonwealth Games	mid-July
Wisconsin	Badger State Games	late June
Wyoming	Cowboy State Games	early June

Education Level

Unlike most European nations, where clubs and municipalities own and manage track facilities, it is the American school systems (high schools, junior colleges, colleges, and universities) that control the facilities. A majority of U.S. high schools sport a track-and-field team, and most have their own tracks, complete with jumping pits, throwing circles, hurdles, and other equipment. Short of building your own track and field, any use of facilities and equipment for decathlon training and meets must be done with the cooperation and support of the schools and their coaches.

High School Decathlons

The decathlon is not a common event at the high school level, but it is gaining popularity and support. In 1994, 13 states offered a state high school decathlon championship to their athletes. Although the other 37 states did not, there does seem to be a movement by many state high school associations to begin to offer a decathlon either as an invitational in the middle of the spring season or as a championship event at the end of it. One stumbling block seems to be that since the javelin is not contested in some states, authorities are reluctant to offer an event that includes it. Some states have overcome this complication by

Courtesy of the Dan O'Brien Youth Foundation

More than a dozen states offer a high school championship decathlon.

offering a javelin clinic or instruction (including safety procedures) as part of the decathlon event, usually immediately before it. Signed waivers are also used.

The javelin problem encourages some states to offer a decathlon while substituting another event for the javelin. Alabama Arkansas, and Tennessee substitute the triple jump.

The states that offered a high school decathlon in 1994 were:

Alabama	Florida	Texas
Arkansas	Montana	Vermont
Arizona	New Hampshire	Virginia
California	Tennessee	Washington
Connecticut		

I suggest that you contact your state high school association for more details. If a decathlon is not offered, you might encourage school officials to do so and even propose to host it yourself. It will be fun, and this is how most decathlon meets have started. A few scholastic leagues also put on a high school decathlon. There are at least four regional scholastic decathlons around the nation:

Brigham Young Invitational
(held early May)
c/o BYU PE Services, RB 112
Provo, UT 84602
801-378-3994

Great SouthWest Decathlon
(held in late May)
Ed Hedges, c/o Central High School
4525 N. Central
Phoenix, AZ 85012
602-274-8100

Glendale Invitational
(early April)
Carol Torrance
3412 W. Glenrose
Phoenix, AZ 85017
602-336-2934

New England High School
(early July)
John Buckley
14 Stagecoach Road
Hingham, MA 02043
617-749-1308

The most exciting development at the scholastic level in recent years has been the establishment of a National High School Invitational Decathlon sponsored by the Dan O'Brien Youth Foundation and Visa, U.S.A. Scholastic decathletes are invited on the basis of their performances at the established meets listed above, as well as their perceived potential. Held in Klamath Falls, OR, Dan O'Brien's hometown, the first two affairs (1994-95) were major successes. The meet is normally held during the first week of July. For more information contacts can be made with the Dan O'Brien Youth Foundation over the Internet:

http://www.danobrien.com/

Many of today's decathletes got their start by doing a scaled-down multi-event, perhaps a pentathlon. The National Indoor Scholastic Championships are held each March at the Carrier

Dome on the campus of Syracuse (NY) University. For more information and entry blanks contact:

Tracy Sundlun
c/o Metropolitan Assn of USA T&F
57 Reade Street
New York, NY 10007-1821
Tel: 212-227-0071

Junior College Decathlons

Many two-year junior or community colleges offer a track program. The National Junior College Athletic Association (NJCAA) has conducted a decathlon as part of its national championships since 1973. Some of the JC districts/states (*e.g.* Arizona) also have a decathlon meet. Since the California junior colleges do not fall under the sway of the NJCAA, they conduct their own championship decathlon (since 1970) every May, following north and south regional qualifiers every April.

Colleges/Universities

Much of the opportunity for American decathletes comes via the university program. Decathlon competitions strictly for college students date to the mid-1920s. The Kansas Relays is the longest continuously running multi-event meet for collegians.

The progressive NAIA, a national organization of smaller colleges, initiated a national decathlon for its members in 1969, and Jeff Bennett of Oklahoma Christian College was its first winner. Indeed, many top decathletes seemed to come from smaller schools where they were in demand in a variety of events.

A year later the NCAA made the decathlon a part of its national program both at the college division (smaller) and university division (larger) championships. Steve Gough (Seattle Pacific) and Rick Wanamaker (Drake U.) were the original titlists. In 1974 the University Division was renamed Division I and the

College Division split into Divisions II (offering scholarships) and III (without scholarships). The automatic entry standards for each divisional meet are adjusted slightly each year. In 1995 they were: I-7750 points; II-6850 points; III-6380 points. Provisional standards are also announced in order to fill a field of 16 to 18 athletes.

Numerous opportunities are available to the collegiate decathlete. Today more than two dozen collegiate conferences offer a decathlon (the first being the Pacific Coast AA, now Big West, in 1970 and IC4A in 1973), usually in May. And the number of decathlons conducted as part of a collegiate invitational or relay meet now exceeds 75 annually. Today there is a temptation for the collegiate decathlete to compete in too many meets, not too few.

The college conferences usually conduct indoor pentathlons or heptathlons annually. The movement began with the IC4A in 1980. Now there are as many as 80 indoor pentathlons in the U.S. winter season. The NAIA and NJCAA offer the pentathlon as a championship event. The NCAA does not.

Finally, a few comments. First, the current collegiate arrangement of offering the U.S. nationals soon after the NCAA Division I championships makes it extremely difficult for collegians ever to make the U.S. national decathlon teams. Making top athletes compete in two decathlons nine days apart freezes some collegians out of later top competition. More cooperation between the two groups is necessary to solve this problem. Second, on a more happy note, the top two U.S. students are eligible to represent the United States at the Universaide, the World University Games, conducted in August/September of each odd-numbered year (1999-2001-2003).

Ability

The ability level of American decathletes ranges from the mediocre to the elite levels. At the lower range, scores of 4000 and 5000 are common. A score of 7000 points is an entrance to the national level, while scores in excess of 8000 points are world-class. Annually about 70-100 athletes score over 7000 nationwide, and a dozen or so usually surpass 8000.

Open Meets

Qualifying for some meets requires a certain score, while other meets are open. In meets of the latter type it is not unusual to have final scores range 3000 points apart. Finding an open meet for the beginner has, at times proved frustrating. But you need to search conscientiously. And you may have to travel. I tell beginners to search out summer decathlons, State Games, and state and USA T&F district meets.

Many meets conduct several divisions: college, junior college, high school, and open. A good beginner's meet has always been the winter meet held each December at California State University at Long Beach. Upwards of 100 athletes compete in five divisions. There are no entry standards. The longest continuously offered decathlon with reasonable standards is the Mount Sac Relays (and accompanying California Invitational) held at Azusa Pacific University each April. Hint: one way to gain acceptance at some meets is to bring along some officials.

Sub-Elite Meets

"Sub-elite" is a new term that applies to those decathletes who score over 7000 points during the spring season but who are unable to meet the high standard necessary to compete in the U.S. nationals (usually in the 7750- to 7800-point range). Once the spring season ends, many of these national-level decathletes lack high-level competitions. USA T&F has, on occasion, sponsored a national sub-elite championship in mid-July.

Courtesy of Iris Hensel

No American stayed at the elite level longer than Kip Janvrin, above,
who competed in over 70 decathlons from 1983-2000.

Elite Meets

The United States has offered a national championship virtually
every year since 1915. Dave Johnson, Dan O'Brien, and Chris
Huffins have dominated U.S. decathlon competition since 1989.
The entry standard score is high (7900 points for 2000).

The top three finishers normally qualify for a major international
via the U.S. championships. At present the international calendar
offers Olympic Games every fourth year, Pan American Games
each pre-Olympic year, the IAAF World Championship each

Courtesy of Millsport

Elite-level decathlons abound. Houston native Drew Fucci
was the 1995 USOC Olympic Festival champion.

odd-numbered year, and the Goodwill Games each even-
numbered non-Olympic year (this may change after 2000). For
example:

1996	26th Olympic Games	Atlanta, GA
1997	6th IAAF World Championships	Athens, Greece

1998	4th Goodwill Games	Uniondale, NY
1999	7th IAAF World Championships	Seville, Spain
1999	Pan American Games	Winnipeg, Canada
2000	27th Olympic Games	Sydney, Australia

There are two major international invitationals that attract the world's best decathletes. Every American elite decathlete should try to compete, at least once in his career, in Götzis, Austria, in late May. Set in the Austrian Alps near the Swiss border, the Götzis decathlon meeting is a quality affair with large, friendly crowds and spectacular scenery. Several world records have been set there. It is worth the trip. And, every September, DecaStar in Talence, set in the wine country of southwestern France, invites the top dozen decathletes worldwide. Both Götzis and Talence have become part of the IAAF Combined Events Grand Prix circuit. Unfortunately for American decathletes, the U.S. nationals and Götzis are but two weeks apart, making for a demanding double.

In recent years Americans have offered a high-quality international invitational, usually in April in California, called DecaJam. If successful, it will eventually become part of the IAAF Grand Prix circuit.

The goal of representing your nation in an international championship is incentive enough for the hours, weeks, and years of training. As they say, there is plenty of room at the top. And Uncle Sam's decathletes have had a good deal of success in recent years, winning the past three World Championships, the past three Goodwill Games, the most recent two Pan American Games, a bronze medal at the 1992 Olympic Games in Barcelona, a gold medal at the Atlanta Olympic Games, and a bronze medal at the 1999 IAAF World Championships in Seville.

Visa, U.S.A. Decathlon Team

In early 1990 credit card giant Visa, U.S.A. announced its backing of a Gold Medal Athlete Program and conducted its first decathlon training clinic at San Francisco State University. It featured the Sports Science Division of the U.S. Olympic Training Center from Colorado Springs, CO, in which decathletes were videotaped, tested, and analyzed in a variety of events.

At the 1990 U.S. nationals the initial ten-man Visa, U.S.A. national decathlon team was selected. Visa provided training stipends, travel allowance, and coaching support for team members for one year. The top ten finishers at each U.S. championship make up the Visa national team.

The program was sanctioned by the U.S. Olympic Committee and track's governing body, USA T&F. Since 1991 two clinics (spring and fall) have been held annually. Athletes are provided physiological and psychological testing, training opportunities, nutrition advice, and the expertise of the nation's leading coaches. The six living American gold medalists—

> Bob Mathias   1948 & 1952 Olympic champion
> Milt Campbell 1956 Olympic champion
> Rafer Johnson 1960 Olympic champion
> Bill Toomey   1968 Olympic champion
> Bruce Jenner   1976 Olympic champion
> Dan O'Brien   1996 Olympic champion

—attend each clinic and provide much-needed experience and invaluable counsel for the team members.

Visa has also offered support for developmental decathlon meets and conceived an annual Visa CUP meeting, a dual-team match between the United States and Germany, which itself has a national club, Team Zehnkampf.

Visa, U.S.A. made the decathlon the very first track event to have corporate support. Its objective has been to keep outstanding athletes training in their post-collegiate days.

Courtesy of Millsport

Visa, U.S.A.has supported a national decathlon team assisted by U.S. Olympic decathlon champions (left to right): Bruce Jenner, Bill Toomey, Rafer Johnson, Milt Campbell, and Bob Mathias. Dan O'Brien (not shown) is the sixth living U.S. gold medalist.

Unfortunately, in 1999 Visa announced its discontinuance of its support, and the decathlon community is now seeking similar support elsewhere.

Individuals with Disabilities

There are a variety of multi-event opportunities for athletes with disabilities. Each of the organizations bases its rules on official USA T&F rules, making modifications only as necessary to accommodate the particular method of competition. A USA T&F Competition Rule Book may be obtained by contacting:

USA Track and Field
One RCA Dome, Suite 140
Indianapolis, IN 46225
Tel: 317-261-0500
Fax: 317-261-0481

Deaf Athletes

Although handicapped in hearing the starter's pistol, deaf athletes have made remarkable progress in recent years. Andrew Herman, son of 1964 U.S. Olympic decathlete Paul Herman, has scored over 7000 points and is the current American Deaf record holder. Even more impressive and indicative of the capabilities of deaf decathletes has been the contemporary performance of Australia's deaf decathlete Dean Smith, who competed in the 1992 Barcelona Olympic decathlon and placed 19th with 7703 points. He has a lifetime best of 7964 points. Deaf athletes use the normal IAAF scoring tables.

Every four years an International Games for the Deaf (which includes a decathlon) is contested, and U.S. teams have fared well. Selection trial meets are conducted. For more information contact the American Athletic Association of the Deaf (AAAD, formerly DAFUS):

>Executive Director
>American Athletic Association of the Deaf (AAAD)
>3607 Washington Blvd., # 4
>Ogden, UT   84403-1737
>Tel: 801-393-7916
>Fax: 801-393-2263

or your state school for the deaf.

Gallaudet University in Washington, DC, has a long-established record of track-and-field accomplishments. Gallaudet's outstanding longtime coach, Tom Berg, is now retired, but for years he worked tirelessly to put his college on the track map. As a result, Gallaudet today stands as a model of what deaf athletes (and decathletes) can accomplish. In recent years, Don Boyer, a high school track coach in western Maryland has served as the decathlon coach for the U.S. deaf teams, which compete internationally. For more information you may want to contact either:

Jack Mika
Track Coach
Gallaudet University
800 Florida Avenue, N.E.
Washington, DC 20002
Tel: 202-651-5603

Don Boyer
7418 Mason Drive
Middletown, MD 21769
Donboyer@aol.com

Blind Athletes

There are currently three classifications of blind athletes: B1, B2, and B3. Without getting technical, they range from athletes who have no light perception in either eye (B1) to best vision of 20/600 (B2) to best vision of 20/200 (B3). Annual competitions are conducted by the United States Association of Blind Athletes (USABA), and current USA T&F rules apply with certain modifications. The USABA offers pentathlon events for men and women. For men, the events are 100 meters, 1500 meters, long jump, javelin, and discus. The International Blind Sports Association (ISBA) provides scoring tables.

For more information on opportunities for athletes who are blind contact:

Dr. Roger Neppi, Executive Director
United States Association of Blind Athletes (USABA)
33 North Institute Street
Brown Hall, Suite 015
Colorado Springs, CO   80903
Tel: 719-630-0422
Fax: 719-630-0616

Special Olympics

Mentally handicapped athletes also have multi-event opportunities via the Special Olympics movement. Today a pentathlon is conducted at the quadrennial Special Olympic World Games and at annual national and regional Special

Olympics competitions. The SO pentathlon is the first day of the decathlon: 100 meters, long jump, shot put, high jump, and 400 meters. It is recommended that the Special Olympics pentathlon be conducted over two days, with the first three events held on the first day and the remaining two events on the second day. Some years back I wrote the Special Olympics pentathlon scoring tables. They are printed in the SO track-and-field handbook and available from:

> Director of Track and Field
> Special Olympics International
> 1350 New York Avenue, N.W.
> Suite 500
> Washington, D.C. 20005
> Tel: 202-628-3630
> Fax: 202-737-1937

Three Final Observations

First, some thought should be given to moving the USA T&F nationals back a few weeks to take care of the collegian (NCAA) problem and to give American decathletes an opportunity to compete at Götzis and a chance at IAAF Grand Prix rewards. One helpful proposal suggests that the United States could combine its elite, sub-elite, and junior national meets, for both decathlon and heptathlon, into a multi-event festival in late June. Other nations do this successfully. The evidence: large crowds and big scores. The benefit: the entire multi-event community gets together once per year. This proposal is heartily endorsed.

Second, two track calendars are available. Click the "Schedule" button at the popular Web site www.decathlonusa.org. A calendar (not perfect) presents lists, dates, sites, contacts, and phone numbers for directors of over 150 U.S. multi-event meets. It could be useful at a variety of levels in planning your competition schedule.

And USA T&F publishes a fabulous Annual Athletics Calendar. Contact:

Press Information Department
USA T&F
P.O. Box 120
Indianapolis, IN 46206
Tel: 317-261-0500

Or check the calendar button on the Web site www.usatf.org.

Third, with decathlon opportunities at a variety of levels, it is possible that those starting out still will be in need of meets. Decathlon meets are still hard to find in late summer and early fall (when weather is ideal). And many meets are closed to collegians or have entry standards. What to do? May I suggest you...

Start a Decathlon Meet

You'll need a facility and equipment, a half-dozen athletes, a handful of experienced officials, a scoring table, and lots of energy. If you do not have experience organizing a decathlon, don't worry. No one else does either. Your meet will be as official as anyone's. And every meet had to start sometime. Who knows, your meet may become an annual affair, and like most others, a labor of love for those who organize it. The athletes will appreciate your efforts and will return to either compete or officiate in the future.

Don't worry about making mistakes. Snafus occur even at our national championship meets.

Just do it. Good luck.

5

Clothing and Equipment

The most important consideration when selecting training attire is comfort. It is by no means necessary to wear the latest in track fashion or the most expensive shoes. But it is worthwhile to invest in a few items for comfort. Let's take a closer look at what you'll need as you head out to the track.

Apparel for Training

Gym Bag

I suggest that you purchase a gym bag and make certain that it is roomy. Decathletes lug around lots of equipment and clothing. It is the nature of the event that requires them to do so. The more events you are practicing or the more variable the weather, the bigger the tote you'll need. At the track don't leave clothing or equipment lying around. If it is not being used, place it in your bag.

Shoes

A basic pair of well-supported running flats can be your most important investment. After all, you'll be in them more than any other shoes, so look for the essentials: comfort, stability, and support. Your distance training, conditioning, general aerobic (nonsprint) running, warm-ups and warm-downs, even some weightlifting, will likely be done in these shoes. And since half of all decathlon injuries are foot related, obtain a decent pair. Even when the heels or soles wear out, shoe repair shops can rebuild them inexpensively.

Spikes

Decathletes use a lot of footwear, including special event shoes such as high jump shoes, javelin boots, and smooth-soled throwing shoes. Running spikes (length of spikes will be determined by the type of running surface) are worth their weight in gold. They may not be inexpensive, but you'll use them for sprint, hurdle, and even vault training and competition. If you also long jump in them, make sure they are properly and strongly stitched to avoid pushing through or tearing out the toe. If they are not manufactured for long jumping, don't use them for long jumping. Obtain a pair of long jump spikes.

As you get more proficient in each of the events, specialty shoes will make sense. Do not, for example, purchase a pair of javelin boots before you have had lots of javelin training. An expensive pair of javelin boots on a weak thrower is like a costly pair of skis on the beginner's slope. It makes little sense.

In any event, bring all the shoes you'll need, and at least two pairs of socks for every training session.

Shirts/Shorts

Next on the list of essentials is proper fitting shirts and shorts. For practice sessions, they have nothing to do with fashion. Keep half a dozen or more T-shirts handy. You'll be surprised how fast you can go through them. The sleeve length is up to you. If sleeves get in the way of performing throwing events or the weather is hot, use a sleeveless shirt or singlet. Singlets should fit snugly. You don't want to wait while growing into one. Comfort is crucial. Wear whatever feels comfortable, and don't let your attire get in the way of performing the events. Extra-long T-shirts and shorts, while fashionable for basketball, are clumsy and only get in the way of training. The same goes for running shorts. Lightweight nylon shorts are inexpensive and durable. Many decathletes opt for spandex running tights.

Courtesy of Millsport

Comfortable clothing is important.

If the weather is cool take along a sweatsuit. If you are just getting started, an inexpensive sweatsuit will be valuable. Most sporting goods stores offer a good selection.

Rain Gear

The use of a two-piece rain suit will be guided by weather in your area. If you run in rain gear, make sure that it fits loosely and is comfortable.

Other Items

It is advisable to leave your jewelry at home. If you wear a nice watch, you may want to purchase an inexpensive sports watch (the kind that can time laps and intervals) to wear around the track. For safety, avoid wearing rings or necklaces. Sunglasses, on the other hand, are often recommended. If you wear them in meets, wear them in practice sessions.

Equipment for Training

In the vast majority of cases, if you're a decathlete, you'll be a member of a track team and have access to the team's equipment. Perhaps it is a high school, junior college, or university. Virtually all the equipment you'll need is standard at most track and field facilities—hurdles, starting blocks, crossbars, pits, and throwing implements.

If you have secured permission to train at a track where you are not a student, you may need to bring equipment that is not readily available. This could include shots, discuses javelins, vaulting poles, and more. Is your gym bag getting heavy?

Before you leave a school's track program (for good or perhaps just for the summer months), find out if there is any equipment that the program can spare—perhaps an old vaulting pole, a broken discus, or a worn-out javelin. But there may come a time,

Courtesy of Victah Sailer

At the higher levels of competition, decathletes use their own vaulting poles.

usually after you decided to pursue a decathlon career, when you may need to purchase some equipment.

In all likelihood this will involve vaulting poles, javelins, and discuses. They are not inexpensive items. Often local sporting goods stores do not stock these items, and they'll have to be obtained from a catalog distributor. Check with the local track coaches, who always seem to have desks littered with these catalogs.

Ask for advice and order with prudence. You won't need a heavy, 16-foot fiberglass vaulting pole if you can barely clear 11 feet. The top-of-the-line javelins are of little use to someone throwing 100 feet.

Once the implements arrive, take proper care of them. Find a special storage area out of the way of family traffic. Poles and javelins ALWAYS should be in carrying cases when not in use. You want to avoid having someone stepping on the unprotected pole and cracking it. Fiberglass vaulting poles need to lie flat, not stand up, when not being used. Transporting them will be your biggest headache. Airlines are infamous for their handling of vaulting poles. More than one airline employee has sawed a pole in half to make it fit a cargo bin! Did you think this was going to be easy?

A good discus should last years. Keep it clean. Avoid nicks by keeping the discus away from concrete. And ONLY throw your discus on grass landing areas. Keep it in a leather carrying case. In most meets you'll be able to use your own throwing implements. At the very highest level, *e.g.*, Olympic Games and World Championships, the meet organizers will supply all throwing implements. In all cases you'll need to use your own vaulting poles.

For practice sessions also bring along an old towel (to wipe off throwing implements), a spiked marker (for long jump and pole vault runway marks), some adhesive tape, extra spikes and spike wrench, small first aid kit, and a water bottle. And bring some sunscreen to avoid getting burned. Many decathletes use a sun protection because of the amount of time they spend outdoors.

Now it's time to grab your cap (for shade) and gym bag and head to the track. The next chapter, on decathlon training, will discuss what to do when you get there.

Apparel and Equipment for Competition

The decathlete must feel confident in his meet preparation. A good mental attitude is served by knowing that he will be self-sufficient for the two days on the field. Whatever the weather, schedule, or situation, the decathlete must have enough clothing and equipment to survive both the small problems (like losing a spike) to the large ones (like breaking a vaulting pole).

A checklist should be consulted several days before the competition, so that items can be prepared or replaced. By circumventing last-minute emergencies you'll be able to stay focused on the competition itself. Then pack your bag the day *before* the meet and check each item again. The following is not an exhaustive list of what you need to pack, but it is a useful one.

CHECKLIST:

throwing implements (if not provided)

vaulting poles (most decathletes bring 2 or more)

folding chair (preferably with low base)

umbrella (the larger the better)

Bag:

measuring tape (for HJ, LJ, PV steps)

markers (LJ & PV)

several towels

small first aid kit

adhesive tape

drinks and snacks

2 pairs of socks for each day

2 pairs of shorts

2 singlets

2-3 T-shirts

more drinks and snacks

sweatsuit

rain suit

running spikes

extra shoelaces

event shoes (Jav, LJ, HJ, throws)

hat or cap

sunglasses

extra spikes and spike wrench

sunscreen

headset and audiotapes

Knowing that you have conscientiously outfitted yourself with all the practical requirements of a decathlon will put you in a confident frame of mind. Now all you must deal with are the ten events. One final suggestion: You might want to pack a conversion table if you are unfamiliar with the metric system. But try to stay away from the scoring tables during the meet. Too many athletes run to the tables after every event. Scoring is someone's else's job. You need to concentrate on DOING the events, not fretting about the scores.

6

Decathlon Training

Before we talk of specific training needs or training for individual events, it is important to address three concepts:

- Recovery
- Balance
- Technique

It is essential for coach and athlete alike to understand that improvement in athletic performance is the result of both training and *recovery*. Hard training, in and of itself, will simply fatigue the body. The body's natural response to hard training is to rebuild weary muscles stronger than before. This rebuilding is done in the recovery phase of training. The length of the recovery phase depends on the amount of stress placed on the body during training.

Overview of Training

The amount of physical work a young athlete can handle will be unique to the individual and depend on factors such as age, physical development, training background, and work ethic. All must be taken into account in arranging a training program for an event as rigorous as the decathlon. But please remember it is necessary that recovery and rest (R&R) be built into the training schedule. It makes no sense to do a workout so strenuous that you are unable to train the next day.

It is clear that a balanced performance, and so *balance* in training, is an ideal that needs careful and diligent planning. Decathlons are rarely won with one or two terrific events. But they are certainly lost with one poor one. Balanced training requires a long time commitment. Remember, training for many of the decathlon events, for example, the shot put (with a focus on power) and the 1500-meter run (with a focus on endurance), cannot occur together. If one wants to be the world's best shot putter, one needs little to no endurance training. And to maximize one's potential in an endurance event, shot put drills are unnecessary. But if one desires to be a multi-event athlete, a decathlete, some of both forms of training are desirable. Balance in training must seek a compromise between the two.

The concept of balance is not an end in itself. Perfect balance, for example, the same number of points in each event, won't win any decathlons. Scoring points will. So remember, scoring is the goal. Don't lose sight of it. A good example in which balance in training is secondary deals with what I call "disaster events." The hurdles (where spills are frequent), the pole vault (where failure to clear the opening height occasionally occurs), and the discus (where three throws landing outside the sector is not uncommon) can all result in a zero score. The first priority should be to practice for dependability and confidence in these events, even though other events might be weaker.

Sound *technique* should be given primary emphasis in training, especially at the beginner's stage. Maturity will enhance a young decathlete's speed, power, and endurance. But flawless technique does not occur naturally. Sam Adams, the longtime track coach at the University of California at Santa Barbara, puts it this way: "the decathlon is the art of executing correctly." Many a decathlete has eliminated himself by throwing the discus outside the throwing sector, or by crashing in the hurdles, or by missing

Courtesy of Millsport

Young decathletes study pole-vault techniques with Washington State
University's coach Rick Sloan, a 1968 Olympic decathlete.

low heights in either the high jump or pole vault, all because of
a deficiency in technique. Much technique is picked up in the
early teen years, as early as junior high school. It should be
biomechanically sound. If not, it needs to be unlearned, then
relearned. This is time consuming and disrupting. Olympic
decathlon medalist Ken Doherty tells us that for athletes who
intend to make a career of the decathlon, no learning is far better
than learning poor technique.

The Fundamentals of Training

A sensible decathlon training program should include the
following elements.

Technique

The goal here is to find a simple, mechanically sound technique
suited to the athlete. The greatest emphasis should come in the
earlier years when motor patterns are developed.

Speed

Many decathlon events are directly related to speed, and speed training can be carried out year-round. Obviously, the intensity of the drills and workouts increases in season and in preparation for competitions. A series of sprints over 30, 60, 100, and 150 meters is common. Use adequate rest before the next sprint. Sprint form drills and practicing the start are also crucial.

Speed Endurance

This applies mainly to 400-meter training, but it has some carryover to both the 1500 and 100 meters. The emphasis is, with good sprint form and body carry, to maintain the developed speed over longer distances. Various combinations of runs at 200, 250, 300, 400, 500, and 600 meters can be used.

Strength Training

Early in a decathlete's career, a general strength training program, which uses traditional weightlifting exercises, should be emphasized. Olympic lifts, such as the snatch and clean and jerk, and power lifts, such as the bench press and half-squat, can be used. These workouts stress the improvement of total overall body strength. The novice or beginner decathlete may start by limiting his general strength training to a circuit on a Universal Gym or similar apparatus.

Specific strength training is aimed at developing power in throwing, jumping, and running. These specific excercises are dynamic attempts to imitate the event movements, and can include medicine ball drills, bounding, hopping, and jumping over hurdles.

General strength training should overshadow specific training in the early stages of a career. Once the athlete reaches proficiency in most events, strength training can be split between general and specific. Never underplay the importance of general strength training. At the same time, make sure that you don't overdo it.

The idea with weightlifting is not to build bulk, but to enhance strength. Decathletes don't enter Mr. America contests. They compete in decathlons. And to do so successfully, their strength training must be a corollary to technique workouts.

Just a word of caution about weightlifting. Never lift alone. Always have a spotter, a friend, another decathlete, someone who will lift with you. This is important both for safety and for motivational reasons.

Endurance Training

The purpose of this type of training is to allow the decathlete to run a solid 1500 meters by developing an aerobic base and to provide the stamina needed to endure the long hours of decathlon competition. This can be accomplished in the off-season by faithful and frequent runs of 20-30 minutes, perhaps three times a week. Adding a 20-30 minute special running workout (fartlek) session once each week during the off-season should be adequate. During the competitive season several paced efforts at 800, 1000, 1100, or 1200 meters are advisable and a confidence builder.

It is not necessary to become a distance runner. But remember: a national-class athlete in satisfactory condition should always be able to run the equivalent of a 5:00 mile, or a 4:40 1500 meters. And at six points for every one-second improvement, the 1500-meter event cannot be ignored.

Flexibility Training

Often overlooked, this is an important ingredient of training. It not only assists in preventing injuries but aids technique by allowing a greater range of motion. *EVERY* workout should be preceded by a 15-20 minute stretching session.

Training Cycles

Some decathletes like to use training cycles in which all the events are practiced. The 21-day, 14-day, and 1-week cycles are common, and vary in intensity depending on the time of year. In-season activities focus on refining speed and speed endurance and perfecting technique. Out-of-season activities feature more work with endurance and strength. All activities feature flexibility.

Here is a sample 14-day cycle for a novice or veteran decathlete. It is a general plan. One would expect the seasoned decathlete to emphasize a more intense work load (longer workouts, heavier lifts, more repetitions, faster runs). Remember, this is just a sample, and each decathlete needs to build his own training cycle:

Sample Training Cycle

For: In-season, competitive season

Length: 14 days

Level: Novice to Veteran

Day 1   Sprinting, LJ, SP, evening strength

Day 2   HH, Disc, PV, 400m training

Day 3   Weak events, evening strength

Day 4   Sprinting (starts), SP, HJ

Day 5   HH, PV, Jav, 400m training

Day 6   General strength training

Day 7   Rest

Day 8   Sprinting, SP, HJ, evening strength

Day 9   HH, PV, Jav, 400m training

Day 10   LJ, SP, 1500m training, strength

Day 11   HH, PV, 400m training

Day 12   Light warmup or general strength

Day 13   Competition in 3-5 events

Day 14   Rest

Note: In preparation for a decathlon on the 13th-14th day of a 14-day cycle, the volume of work is reduced starting with day 8. On day 8 or 9 a fast 300m is advised. On days 9 or 10 some short sprint work would be useful. Days 11 and 12 should be light, perhaps some technique work or active rest.

Sequence Training

You may have noticed that, in the sample training cycle session above, many of the events were practiced in sequence—that is, in the order in which they competitively occur in a decathlon. For example, the discus is practiced after the hurdles, and the pole vault after the discus, just the way they occur on competition day. The idea is to condition the body as it moves from one event to the next. For example, if your legs are always wobbly after the hurdles, it is important to simulate that feeling in practice by throwing the discus after a hurdles workout. This conditions the athlete to make the transition from one event to the next.

The late Estonian (and Soviet) decathlon coach Fred Kudu suggests that decathletes not be married to the concept of sequence training. But for some athletes it could be useful. Far more important is to train for technique and speed at the onset of the training session, with jumping in the middle, and strength and endurance at the end of a session.

A Few Notes about Training for the Novice

Beginning decathletes will vary greatly in age, ability, interest, and experience. The problems faced by the 15-year-old high school sophomore, the 21-year-old college junior, or the 44-year-old beginner Masters decathlete will also show significant variations. Some decathletes may have years of track-and-field experience, others little to none. But their basic goal is the same: to complete all ten events with a satisfying feeling and the hope of competing in future decathlons.

Because of the demands of the decathlon, the training load will be heavy. To prevent injuries and keep a fresh attitude, I suggest a few training tips:

1. Plan an adequate amount of rest. Plan rest days or easy days. The only things you accumulate by trying to work out while feeling lethargic are injuries.

2. Have at least one training partner. Few are the great decathletes who train alone. At times it's just nice to have someone to talk with. And never, NEVER vault alone.

3. Alter your training site. Occasionally go to another track, another golf course, another weight room. With all the demands of decathlon training, it is easy to fall into a tedious routine.

4. On any given day do sprint and technique work before any speed endurance workout. Endurance and power training should be done at the end of the session, not before. Don't do a long run or a weightlifting session, then come to the track to sprint or vault or hurdle. It's a good way to wind up injured. Sprint and technique work must be done while you are fresh.

5. If you have advanced to the stage of using a training cycle (discussed above), technique work should follow a rest day or easy training day. Speed and speed endurance should be placed in the middle of the cycle, with endurance and strength work place near the end.

6. Don't ignore weak events.

7. Don't be afraid to experiment.

8. Don't sacrifice training for indoor or early season results.

9. Sometimes less is more. If you are tired, err on the conservative

side and call it a day. The number of injuries caused by and to decathletes is almost epidemic. You have heard and seen it before. "Let's do one more repeat," or "Why don't you take one more throw?" Injuries result and careers are altered or ended by coaches who want you to train until *they* get tired. Set a predetermined number of efforts, do them, then stop. Use common sense.

10. Keep records of your training sessions. A small log book or notebook will do. They will be valuable in the future in putting together a training regime or just to see what you did right before that big breakthrough.

Courtesy of Millsport

Training partners can offer support, advice, competition, and sympathy.

Additional notes: For viewpoints in this chapter I am indebted to Ken Doherty, Ph.D., whose *Track and Field Omnibook* (Tafnews Press, Los Altos, CA, 4th ed.) is the bible for much track-and-field training. It should be consulted for more detailed aspects of training for each of the individual decathlon events. Doherty was an Olympic decathlon medalist, national decathlon champion, longtime coach at both Michigan and Pennsylvania, meet director of the Penn Relays, and the sport's most prolific writer. He is an inductee of the National Track and Field Hall of Fame.

I have drawn upon the work of a pair of former decathletes, Gordon Stewart (former Canadian record holder) and Vern Gambetta (former editor of *Track Technique*), for elementary training cycles. See "Decathlon Training: From Beginner to Master," *Track Technique* # 70, December 1977, p. 2219.

7

Doing Your First Decathlon

The first intention of the beginner is to *complete* the entire ten events. FINISH. If there is a concern that you might not finish your first (or any decathlon), don't start. With this in mind it may be advisable for a beginner to tackle a few one-day pentathlons (indoors or out) before going to a full decathlon.

The standard indoor pentathlon consists of 60-meter hurdles, long jump, shot put, high jump, and 1000-meter run. The outdoor pentathlon is also standard: long jump, javelin, 200 meters, discus, 1500-meter run. Even a triathlon, consisting of any run, jump, or throw (*e.g.* hurdles, high jump, javelin), will be useful. In any event it will be important for the novice to compete (against others or a stop watch or measuring tape) in the pole vault, hurdles, discus, and javelin in the weeks prior to the first decathlon. It will be important at least to score in these troublesome and exacting events.

In the first decathlon it is vital that the novice achieve some point score, be it ever so modest, in each event. It is therefore important that he establish some sort of rough technique in the four aforementioned events. In the hurdles it is important to try to establish three steps between hurdles for as long as possible.

If one has to drop to five, so be it. The author remembers one high school athlete who alternated and took four strides between hurdles. Not recommended. In the pole vault it is best to use a short run, perhaps in the 10- to 15-stride range with a low top hand hold (9 to 10 feet). In the discus the athlete should adjust his starting position in the circle to ensure a fair landing. And in the javelin a short (perhaps 5 or 7 step), controlled approach will likely provide a decent throwing position and toss.

Courtesy of the Dan O'Brien Youth Foundation

In your first decathlon, it's important to score in every event.

Use a conservative (in terms of steps) approach in the long jump on the first effort to guarantee a legal mark. There is a good case for taking at least one jump at a low height in both the high jump and pole vault, no matter what the athlete's background in these events. It takes little energy, and any step problems can be resolved at the lower heights. And, of course, there is also the psychological satisfaction that at least one height has been cleared. At no time, when approaching PR heights, should a decathlete pass a height.

Courtesy of the Dan O'Brien Youth Foundation

Personal record (PR) vault clearances occur frequently
in early competitions.

In terms of the 1500 meters, even though the novice may have little to no background at anything longer than, say, 400 meters, it would be useful in the weeks leading up to the first decathlon to repeat some occasional 400-meter runs in 80 seconds or 800-meter runs in 2:40 to establish the pace of a five-minute 1500 meters. The author can recall a novice collegiate decathlete with 47+ second 400-meter skills running the first 400 of a 1500 in 61+ seconds, then spending the next four minutes running in sand. His was a short career.

OK, let go to the first meet. Suffice to say that the beginner athlete will arrive with adequate shoes and clothing to take into account the possibility of bad weather. Ample snacks and fluids are also important. The decathlete must be self-sufficient in terms of equipment. Nothing must disturb his poise.

Every event must be preceded by a specific warm-up: stretching, jogging, striding, sprinting, hurdling, jumping, throwing; whatever the event dictates. There should be no attempt to let the warm-up for the previous event serve for the following event.

Don't carry over failures from the preceding event. Only carry over successes. Forget the failures and get on with the next discipline. And, finally, stay off your feet when not warming up. Part of the decathlon game is managing your energy.

The first meet will be valuable, for you will learn from the experience and be able to evaluate your strengths and weaknesses. One way to do so is to make notes of each meet. A simple notebook will do with the sort of form provided below. Wait until the meet or day is over and write your comments out. Now you have a record of them. In the future they will be invaluable. Here is a sample:

PERSONAL DECATHLON RECORD

Name of Meet:

Site: Date:

This is my   decathlon; PR score:

Event	PR	Performance	Points	Comments
100m				
LJ				
SP				
HJ				
400m				
1st day points total				

110mH				
Disc				
PV				
Jav				
1500m				
2nd day points total				

Total Score: Place: Winner:

Perhaps that first record sheet will look like this:

PERSONAL DECATHLON RECORD

Name of Meet:

Site: Date:

This is my   decathlon; PR score:

Event	PR	Performance	Points	Comments
100m				
LJ				
SP				
HJ				
400m				
1st day points total				
110mH				
Disc				
PV				
Jav				
1500m				
2nd day points total				

Total Score: **Place:**   **Winner:**

This score of 4838 points is a good one. Why? Because the first success in the decathlon is to complete it. In your first meet I wonder how many did not do so! Don't worry that the score is 4000 points shy of the current world record. Dan O'Brien, who used to hold that record, recorded a 4643 total in his very first decathlon as a Klamath Falls, OR, high school freshman. As you can see, he has made considerable progress. And Bill Toomey's first decathlon (in 1959) netted him just 5349 points. Nine years later he was the Olympic champion, and a year after that the world-record holder with 8417 points. So you see, any score is a good one for the first decathlon. Just complete it.

Toomey, now an articulate motivational speaker, likens starting the decathlon to looking up a long flight of steps. Climbing those steps won't be easy, but what you discover at each new elevation is that the view gets better, it improves and is a cause of satisfaction. "Don't put a lid on what you can achieve," says Toomey. "Just take one step at a time and use setbacks productively. Learn. The decathlon is like golf. Your next stroke could be your best one. And don't be overly concerned about how fast you move up those steps. Some guys are on escalators, while others have to take it one step at a time."

So learn from your first and each decathlon. Toomey concludes, "Every day in the decathlon you have a chance to be better than you've ever been before." After your first completed decathlon you'll already be making plans for the next one.

8

Nutrition, Health Hazards, and First Aid

Those of us who are active in the training and promotion of the decathlon share a twin objective of assisting athletes to maximize their competitive performance, while at the same time protecting their health and welfare. This chapter deals with the correlation between nutrition and performance, and the serious issues of health and injury.

Nutrition

Diet significantly sways athletic performance. For anyone interested in the decathlon, an adequate diet before, during, and after both training and competition will maximize effectiveness. In the optimum diet for the decathlon, carbohydrates are likely to contribute about 60-70 percent of total energy intake, and protein about 15-20 percent, with the remainder coming from fat.

Carbohydrates are sugars and starches found in grain and grain products (cereals, bread, rice, pasta), fruits, vegetables, milk and dairy products, and many processed foods and drinks. *Proteins* are the body's building blocks needed for growth and repair of damaged cells. Proteins help digestion and fight infection. The major sources of protein are meats, fish, milk and dairy products, eggs, and nuts. *Fats* are a concentrated source of food energy, help build body tissues and contain the fat-soluble vitamins A, D, E, and K. Saturated fats are found in red meats, whole eggs, whole milk, and milk products. Unsaturated fats are found in nuts and many vegetable oils. Although fat is essential in the diet, nutritionists recommend that fat should provide no more than 10-20 percent of an athlete's energy intake. A note of caution: animal products (for example, red meat) are not the only sources of protein and fat. Some world-class athletes follow a low-fat diet composed mostly of plant foods.

We also need a wide range of vitamins and minerals. A varied diet can provide our normal requirements; supplements may be valuable but are no replacement for an adequate diet. Water and fiber are also essential. Decathletes need to drink extra water.

A Guide to Daily Food Choices

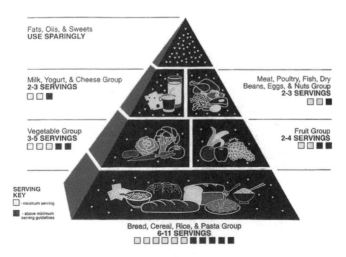

Source: U.S. Department of Agriculture and the
U.S. Department of Health and Human Services

Courtesy of Millsport

Proper nutrition helps supply the power for the three throwing events.

Decathletes need more energy than normal. The more active you are, the more energy you need. Decathletes use 5,000 or more calories a day. Where should this extra energy come from? Scientific research show that it is important to get this extra energy by increasing carbohydrate intake, rather than by eating more protein or fat.

In summary, a healthy diet is one that provides the energy we need from the correct proportions of nutrients. We should have a wide variety of foods and drinks to ensure that we obtain all the vitamins and minerals we need.

Total energy intake must be raised to meet the increased energy drained during training. Decathletes should always monitor their body weight, body composition (percentage of fat), and food intake. From a diet standpoint, the decathlon is both a power and an endurance event.

Fluid intake should be given at least as much attention as the intake of carbohydrates and other nutrients. All the body cells contain water, and this accounts for 60 percent of body weight. Water is needed for the body's cooling system, transportation of nutrients throughout tissues, and maintenance of adequate blood volume. Dehydration can cause the body to overheat, and even small unreplaced fluid losses can impair performance. Decathletes should not wait until they feel thirsty; in fact, athletes needs to replenish fluids *before* they start feeling thirsty. Because there is a premium on endurance, decathletes should drink water before, during, and after both training and competition. Drink more than you think you should.

A quick word about alcohol. Although enjoyable, consumption of alcohol will do nothing to prevent dehydration. Alcohol is a diuretic; that is, it increases urine formation so that slightly more fluid is lost as urine than will be consumed as alcohol. It therefore increases rather than decreases dehydration. Under no circumstances should a decathlete have a beer during training or competition or between competitive days.

A word of caution about nutritional supplements. Many claim amazing results. Be suspicious. Most nutritional research does not support those claims. In terms of vitamin supplements for young decathletes, unless there is a natural deficiency or the work load is abnormally high, athletes eating a diet adequate both quantitatively and qualitatively will find little need for them.

Health Hazards

Athletes of all ages, but especially young and talented athletes, are subject to an extensive assortment of influences. For many youngsters the desire to accommodate external or internal pressures tempts them to venture into habits that can jeopardize their track career and health.

Smoking

More than a generation ago the U.S. Surgeon General warned all

Americans of the health dangers from smoking. The medical and research evidence on the risks of smoking to one's lungs and its role as a cancer agent seems overwhelming and undeniable to all but the tobacco manufacturers. The reduction of lung capacity in a strong, young athlete is magnified by the fact that tobacco is an addictive drug. In the summer of 1995 the President of the United States called on the domestic tobacco firms to limit their teenage advertising focus. And the adjustment of nicotine levels in cigarettes remains a contentious issue today.

For youngsters who intend to make a career of the decathlon, abstinence from cigarettes is an absolute. Yes, there are world-class athletes (and decathletes) who smoke. I can still recall my amazement at a post-decathlon reception overseas in the 1980s where numerous European decathletes were smoking. To a man, they claimed that smoking would have minimal influence on their conditioning/performance and that it was important to relax after a big meet. There are healthier ways to unwind than by using an addictive drug. Today these decathletes are retired from active competition, but they still smoke.

Smokeless Tobacco

National surveys warn us of the surprising increase in the use of smokeless tobacco by high school and junior high school students. As a college professor I am distressed by the number of students who come to class displaying the smokeless tobacco habit. Perhaps it is peer pressure or the desire to emulate professional athletes.

Whatever the reasons, if you intend to compete in something as strenuous as the decathlon, put all notions of smokeless tobacco products aside. The health repercussions are numerous. Can you spell C-A-V-I-T-Y? Pouch tobacco has a typical sugar content of 35 percent. Soaking teeth in sugar certainly enhances the risk of cavities. Gum disease and tooth loss are not uncommon. The National Institute of Drug Abuse and the American Psychological

Association note that smokeless tobacco can result in a dependent habit. It is a myth that the use of smokeless tobacco will enhance an athlete's (and decathlete's) reaction time to the starter's pistol. It is no myth that the use of smokeless tobacco can have long-term health implications.

Anabolic Steroids

The use of steroid drugs, properly called anabolic-androgenic steroids (AAS), became prominent through the U.S. weightlifting community in the Middle Atlantic states in the late 1950s and early 1960s. The purpose of AAS is to both enhance athletic performance and stimulate muscular development. There is enough evidence to suggest that it does both, but at a heavy price to long-term health.

The consequences of steroid use are so appalling that they easily outnumber any possible performance benefits to the user.

In young boys the use of AAS can result in acne, breast enlargement, hair loss, and yellowing of eyes. Body growth can be stunted. But the negative side-effects of AAS are not just physical. The American Sports Education Institute counsels that there are psychological effects to anabolic steroid use, which may include any of the following: extensive mood swings from raging violence to depression, irritability, jealousy, delusions, and damaged judgment.

Why anyone would risk any or all of the above disorders is a great mystery to sports observers. Yet track and field is still bedeviled by steroids and, in the United States, steroid use among youngsters, athlete and nonathletes alike, is extremely high, perhaps in the millions. The desire for social approval through muscular growth is serious indeed. A sizable portion of young male users are nonathletes who simply desire to look like Tarzan. It has been estimated that sales of illegal steroids in the United States (the substantial fraction via direct mail or gyms) now exceed $400 million annually. That's a lot of steroids, and as a nation, we will pay the price in health problems within the next generation.

The most widely publicized case of steroid misuse involved Canadian sprinter Ben Johnson, who was divested of his 100-meter-dash gold medal after failing a drug test at the 1988 Seoul Olympics. Nationally and internationally a number of decathlon men have been suspended for steroid use. Random, year-round testing at the elite levels is conducted both by USA Track and Field and by the International Amateur Athletic Federation (IAAF). Testing also occurs at the club level and at major meetings and is also conducted by the National Collegiate Athletic Association (NCAA) for its members. Today, at least in track and field, athletes run a heavy risk because of frequent testing. The highly successful Visa U.S.A. decathlon program, initiated in 1990, is a prime example of how team members can be world-class decathletes and drug free.

From an ethical standpoint we should deplore the use of AAS for muscle building or improved athletic performance. We do not want to see athletes become inhuman. It seems silly that athletes would want, and the public accept, better performances through pharmacy.

To learn more about AAS and its effects, I suggest *Anabolic Steroids: Altered States,* by James E. Wright and Virginia S. Cowart. (Benchmark Press, Carmel, IN, 1990.)

Alcohol

Many Americans choose to make drinking beverage alcohol a part of their lives and do so in a responsible manner. For young track-and-field athletes, and decathletes in particular, the question of to drink or not to drink figures prominently in their social acceptance. We have already noted that alcohol consumption has a dehydrating effect on the body. It is also a depressant.

Partly because of societal pressure, many youngsters, athletes included, drink immoderately and run a high risk of alcohol problems, including drunk driving accidents. As long as alcohol is not part of training or competition, and done in moderation, the impact on a decathlon career will be minimal. The same cannot be said for any recreational drug usage. It has no place in sports. Remember, obey the law.

First Aid

Before a youngster begins to train for the decathlon, or any related track-or-field event, a physical examination by a doctor is recommended. Your physician will caution you about overwork and remind you that muscles need to be conditioned.

Train with a partner so that someone will be available if an injury strikes. Much of decathlon activity, both training and competition, is ballistic. Stress on body parts can result in injury. Some common injuries to decathletes are acute strains to:

Hamstring muscles

Quadriceps muscles

Groin muscles

Knees, including hyperextension

Ankles

Shoulder muscles

If there is an injury, ice should be applied immediately and the muscle should be rested. If the injury is serious, a physician should be consulted.

To help prevent injuries, before training a 15- to 20-minute period of stretching is recommended. All muscles to be used should be stretched in a static fashion, that is, holding the stretched position for 5-10 seconds. Ballistic stretching during this phase is not recommended. Muscles are much like rubberbands. They must be slowly stretched, not yanked apart. Don't start your workout until you have completed the stretching phase.

Some athletic injuries are caused by a simple muscle imbalance, for example, between quadriceps and hamstrings. If one set of muscles is significantly stronger than another, muscle pulls will be common. Consult your coach and trainer about tests for muscle imbalance.

In most school situations a trainer is available to care for athletic injuries. But if the athlete is training off-hours, off-season, or without the supervision of a trainer, then a first aid kit should always be carried to the training site, whether it be the track, field, field house, or weight room. The typical contents of a decathlete's first aid kit would include:

- Antibiotic ointment
- Adhesive bandages of various sizes
- Adhesive tape (1 to 2 inches wide)
- Unbroken cold packs
- Elastic bandages
- Scissors
- Bottle of Tylenol or Advil
- Towel
- Utility knife, *e.g.*, a Swiss Army knife
- Several quarters (emergency phone calls)

The items above can be obtained, at a nominal cost, at your local pharmacy. It is always recommended that, taped to the inside of the kit, the athlete keep an insurance form and the phone numbers of physicians and emergency vehicles.

Bring plenty of fluids to any training session or competition. A rule of thumb should be to drink four 8-ounce cups of fluid for every pound of weight lost in exercise. There are many sports drinks available on the market which assist in replacing lost salt, minerals, and other essentials.

Serious injuries—for example, a vaulting accident—are uncommon in decathlon, but it is always better to be prepared. If you believe an athlete's injury to be serious, the following guidelines will help everyone deal successfully with it.

Remain calm. Screaming will not help. It's hard to make decisions when you are upset. Moreover, your behavior may determine the reactions of others around you, including other athletes, officials, parents, and spectators.

Don't move the injured athlete. This could compound the injury. If the athlete is unconscious, make him as comfortable as possible and send for immediate help. Whenever there is any doubt as to the nature or extent of an injury, ask for emergency help.

Under no circumstances should the athlete be allowed to continue the training or competition. Rest is nature's remedy for most injuries.

Athletes and coaches must use common sense about athletic injuries. There is a tendency to try to come back from an injury too quickly, resulting in a more serious injury and perhaps loss of season. For example, hamstring injuries normally sideline an athlete between one and three weeks, depending upon the severity and response to treatment. Make sure the athlete has the whole range of motion and can train without pain before allowing him to compete. If there is a question, err on the side of caution.

For more information about the prevention and cure of athletic injuries, you should refer to any standard text. One is *Sports Medicine: Prevention, Evaluation, Management and Rehabilitation,* by Roy and Irvin (Prentice Hall, Inc., Englewood Cliffs, NJ).

Notes: In the section on nutrition the author has relied on the conclusions of the International Scientific Consensus Conference on Foods, Nutrition and Sports Performance held in February 1991 in Lausanne, Switzerland.

I am indebted to other Guides in the USOC Sports Series, especially the *Basic Guide to Soccer* written by Joey Lorraine Parker, for my sections on both smokeless tobacco and anabolic steroids.

For the section on first aid I am indebted to Colin Provost, trainer at Mount St. Mary's College, for his help in identifying common decathlon injuries.

9

Decathlon Scoring Tables

It has often been said that the most difficult thing about the decathlon is not doing ten events, but understanding the scoring tables. You don't need to understand them. Few people do. But you do have to accept that all sports have constants, and the current IAAF scoring table is the decathlon's constant. Like 10-foot baskets or 90-foot basepaths, the table gives the decathlete a point of reference, of comparison. And, no matter what else is said about the construction of the table (and much is said), it is the same for everyone. In basketball, for example, no matter what the dichotomy of sizes and skills, everyone shoots at the same hoop. Muggsy Bogues and Shaquille O'Neal both aim at a 10-foot rim. So too in the decathlon. Everyone works with the same table. And even if you don't like the tables, a change in the IAAF scoring tables *soon* is as unlikely as raising the baskets to 12 feet. We may as well accept them.

The construction of the scoring tables should have an impact on how the decathlete trains. Each of the event tables has slightly progressive slopes. That is, for each additional constant improvement in performance, more and more points are awarded. As in any other economizing situation, the decathlete wants to maximize points given a fixed amount of resources, namely, time, skill, experience, and work capacity. Each decathlete should examine his own capabilities and stage of development, as well as the tables, to determine which events will be stressed in training. It does not make any sense, for example, for an athlete with great skills as, say, a long jumper, to train long hours to hone that event and receive just a few incremental points, when he could have used a shorter period of time to pick up the same additional points in, say, the 400 meters.

Courtesy of Millsport

**Always designate someone to keep the official score,
as scoring errors are common.**

The stage of development is very important here. Athletes in their early years can easily pick up more than 150 points in the 400 meters by improving from, say, 57.9 to 54.0. Add another 150 points by going from 5:05 to 4:40 in the 1500 meters. The 300 points can be produced without any improvement in skill. Indeed, the 1500 meters appears to be an event that pays big dividends for improved performance. Every additional one-second reduction means another 6 points to your score. Take advantage of it.

I do not intend to persuade decathlon men into forgetting some events in favor of others. Reliance on scoring heavily in a few events no longer results in a decathlon victory. Balance is the key word here, since it is the balanced athlete who finds himself in less trouble if one of his events goes awry, especially if it is one of his better events. He will have other solid events to fall back on.

I suggest that, as a decathlon meet approaches, athletes remain running sharp. There are big points to be gained by incrementally faster times and, conversely, big points to be lost if your speed is not sharp.

Remember, the decathlon is a metric event, so all field events must be measured and scored in meters. You'll need to get moderately familiar with the metric system. You cannot, for example, look up a 6' 0" high jump in the IAAF tables. The events must be measured in meters, and if you want to know the closest imperial conversion, you'll also need a conversion table. Incidentally, 1.83 meters = 6 feet. If you look up 1.83m, you'll find that it is worth 653 points.

Now, what do the tables look like and where can you obtain a copy? Here is a sample of what the tables look like.

Men
High Jump

Meters	Points
1.89	705
1.88	696
1.87	687
1.86	679
1.85	670
1.84	661
1.83	653
1.82	644
1.81	636
1.80	627

The scoring tables are published by the IAAF, but the easiest way to obtain a copy in the United States is via *Track and Field News*. Ask for *Scoring Tables for Men's and Women's Multi-Event Competitions*. I also suggest that those unfamiliar with the metric system (which is just about all of us) obtain a very handy spiral-bound guide from *T&FN* entitled the *Big Green Book*. It contains a conversion table, an *abbreviated* set of scoring tables, and much more useful information. It is invaluable at decathlon competitions. The IAAF tables are also printed in the annual *NCAA Track and Cross Country Men's & Women's Rules*. Addresses:

Track & Field News
2570 El Camino Real, Suite 606
Mountain View, CA 94040
Tel: 415-948-8188
Fax: 415-948-9445

NCAA Publishing
P.O. # 781046
Indianapolis, IN 46778
Tel: 888-388-9748
E-mail:ncaa@sgi-net.com

Here is a summary of the scoring tables:

Event/Points	1000	900	800	700	600	500	400
100 Meters	10.39	10.82	11.27	11.75	12.26	12.81	13.41
Long Jump	7.76m	7.36m	6.95m	6.51m	6.06m	5.59m	5.09m
Shot Put	18.40m	16.79m	15.16m	13.53m	11.89m	10.24m	8.56m
High Jump	2.21m	2.11m	2.00m	1.89m	1.77m	1.65m	1.52m
400 Meters	46.71	49.16	50.32	52.58	54.98	57.57	60.40
110m Hurdles	13.80	14.59	15.41	16.29	17.23	18.25	19.38
Discus	56.18m	51.40m	46.60m	41.72m	36.80m	31.78m	26.68m
Pole Vault	5.29m	4.97m	4.64m	4.30m	3.94m	3.57m	3.18m
Javelin	77.20m	70.68m	64.10m	57.46m	50.74m	43.96m	37.06m
1500 Meters	3:53.79	4:07.42	4:21.77	4:36.96	4:53.20	5:10.73	5:29.96

Here is what the approximate incremental performances are worth:

100 Meters	0.10 sec = 22 pts	or	10 pts = 0.05 sec
Long Jump	10 cm = 24 pts	or	10 pts = 4 cm
Shot Put	50 cm = 30 pts	or	10 pts = 15 cm
High Jump	3 cm = 28 pts	or	10 pts = 1 cm
400 Meters	0.50 sec = 24 pts	or	10 pts = 0.20 sec
110m Hurdles	0.10 sec = 12 pts	or	10 pts = 0.08 sec
Discus	1 meter = 20 pts	or	10 pts = 50 cm
Pole Vault	10 cm = 30 pts	or	10 pts = 3 cm
Javelin	1 meter = 15 pts	or	10 pts = 65 cm
1500 Meters	5 seconds = 34 pts	or	10 pts = 1.5 sec

Here is a very abbreviated metric conversion for the six field events:

Long Jump	Shot Put	High Jump	Discus	Pole Vault	Javelin
5.0m=18-2	10.0m=32-9+	1.6m=5-3	25.0m=82-0	2.5m=8-22	35.0m=114-10
6.0m=19-83	11.0m=36-13	1.7m=5-7	30.0m=98-5	3.0m=9-10	40.0m=131-3
6.5m=21-4	12.0m=39-42	1.8m=5-10+	35.0m=114-7	3.5m=11-5+	45.0m=147-8
7.0m=22-11+	13.0m=42-8	1.9m=6-2+	40.0m=131-3	4.0m=13-12	5.00m=164-0
7.5m=24-73	14.0m=45-11	2.0m=6-6+	45.0m=147-8	4.5m=14-9	55.0m=180-5
8.0m=26-3	15.0m=49-22	2.1m=6-10+	50.0m=164-0	5.0m=16-4+	6.00m=196-10
8.8m=28-102	16.0m=52-6	2.2m=7-22	55.0m=180-5	5.5m=18-2	65.0m=213-3

+ = 3/4 inch

What Are Those Decathlon Points All About?

What Performances Are Necessary to Reach Certain Scores?

Some decathletes may want to know what it takes to score, say, 6000 points—or 7000, 8000, or even 9000. Of course, there is no single answer, since every athlete differs in skill and aptitude. Below you'll find the performance needed to achieve those levels, by scoring 1/10th of the total in each event (for example, 600 points per event, for a total of 6000). This, in itself, may be useful.

	6000 points	7000 points	8000 points	9000 points
100m	12.26	11.75	11.27	10.82
LJ	6.06m	6.51m	6.95m	7.36m
SP	11.89m	13.53m	15.16m	16.79m
HJ	1.77m	1.89m	2.00m	2.11m
400m	54.98	52.58	50.32	48.19
110H	17.23	16.29	15.41	14.59
DT	36.79m	41.72	46.59	51.040
PV	3.94m	4.30m	4.64m	4.97m
JT	50.74m	57.45m	64.09m	70.67m
1500m	4:53.20	4:36.96	4:21.77	4:07.42

What Performances Will It Take to Set a Record ?

On the other hand, you may want to know what it would take to win the Olympic Games, or set an American record, or World record. Below you will find listed the last three decathlon world records. The most recent was set by Tomas Dvorak of the Czech Republic in Prague in 1999. Dan O'Brien's mark is still the American record, and Daley Thompson's 1984 score is still the best ever at the Olympic Games.

1984 Los Angeles - Daley Thompson (8847 points)

100m	LJ	SP	HJ	400m	110H	DT	PV	JT	1500m
10.44	8.01m	15.72m	2.03m	46.97	14.33	46.56m	5.00m	65.24m	4:35.00

Cumulative Points

898	2052	2886	3717	4677	5609	6408	7318	8135	8847

1992 Talence - O'Brien (8891 points)

100m	LJ	SP	HJ	400m	110H	DT	PV	JT	1500m
10.43	8.08m	16.69m	2.07m	48.51	13.98	48.56m	5.00m	62.58m	4:42.10

Cumulative points

992	2073	2967	3826	4720	5697	6537	7447	8224	8891

1999 Prague - Dvorak (8994 points)

100m	LJ	SP	HJ	400m	110H	DT	PV	JT	1500m
10.54	7.90m	16.78m	2.04m	48.08	13.73	48.33m	4.90m	72.32m	4:37.20

Cumulative points

966	2001	2900	3740	4645	5655	6491	7371	8296	8994

Highest Cumulative Score after Each Event

The highest cumulative score ever achieved *after* each of the ten events is listed below:

100
Score:1042   Chris Huffins   Olympic Trials, Atlanta, 1996
Marks: (10.22)

LJ
Score: 2090   Dan O'Brien   TAC, New York, 1991
Marks: (10.23 - 7.96m)

SP
Score: 2967   Dan O'Brien   DecaStar,Talence, 1992
Marks: (10.43 - 8.08m - 16.69m)

HJ
Score: 3838   Dan O'Brien   USATF, Knoxville, 1994
Marks: (10.31 - 7.81m - 15.87m - 2.17m)

400
Score: 4747   Dan O'Brien   TAC, New York, 1991
Marks: (10.23 - 7.96m - 16.06m - 2.08m - 47.70)

110H
Score: 5735   Dan O'Brien   Goodwill, St. Petersburg, 1994
Marks: (10.49 - 7.81m - 15.70m - 2.20m - 47.73 - 13.81)

DT
Score: 6579   Chris Huffins   USATF, New Orleans, 1998
Marks: (10.31 - 7.76m - 15.43m - 2.18m - 49.02 - 14.02 - 53.22m)

PV
Score: 7499   Dan O'Brien   TAC, New York, 1991
Marks: (10.23 - 7.96m - 16.06m - 2.08m - 47.70 - 13.95 - 48.08m - 5.10m)

JT
Score: 8296   Tomas Dvorak   EuroCup, Prague, 1999
Marks: (10.54 - 7.90m - 16.78m - 2.04m - 48.08 - 13.73 - 48.33m -
        4.90m - 72.32m)

1500
Score: 8994   Tomas Dvorak   EuroCup, Prague, 1999
Marks: (10.54 - 7.90m - 16.78m - 2.04m - 48.08 - 13.73 - 48.33m -
        4.90m - 72.32m - 4:37.20)

10

A Few Reminders

For Athletes

- You don't have to be outstanding in any one event to be the champion in the ten events.

- It really doesn't matter if the athlete finishes first, second, third, or worse in a particular event. The score is the thing. At the 1995 IAAF World Championships, Dan O'Brien did not win one event outright, yet won the decathlon by over 200 points. For the most part decathletes compete against themselves while keeping a wary eye on the opposition.

- The decathlon is an event where there is a chance to recuperate from a mistake. Foul up in one event and there is still hope.

- Don't allow failure in one event to spill over to the next event. Think positively. And, please, don't drop out just because things are not going well.

- Be aggressive to the end. Even in the 1500 meters, be greedy and go for as many points as you can possibly run up.

- Be familiar with the rule book.

- Many of the decathlete's psychological problems (nervousness, stress, anxiety) can be resolved by good organization. Good warm-ups are beneficial both physiologically and psychologically. Nothing helps like being prepared.

- The decathlon is the most social of track events and promotes the greatest sense of camaraderie among the contestants. If you offer assistance, advice, or implements, you'll receive the same in return.

- The decathlon is more than a physical test. It is a test of character and attitude. The attitude must always be positive.

- Take pride in the records you set but remember that the only records you *OWN* are personal ones. You don't own world, national, or meet records. You are just holding them until someone else comes along and breaks them. Sooner or later, someone will. Records do not last forever.

- If you don't intend to finish, you shouldn't start.

- Honor your competitors with your best effort. And expect nothing less than their best. Bruce Jenner was fond of saying, "I love my competitors because they bring out the best in me."

- Thank officials after the competition.

For Coaches

- Athletes seldom make a long-term commitment to the decathlon at an early age. Rather, their interest is likely to evolve, especially after some early successes. The coach's responsibility is to nurture that interest.

- Do not expect athletes to set personal records in every event in every meet. I wonder how many potential decathletes have been soured by their coaches expecting too much too soon.

- Summing PRs is no way to project a final score or a "qualifying score." Remember, if you fudge performances/scores on an entry blank, you are taking a spot away from someone more deserving.

- Nothing hurts a meet (and the decathlete) as much as entering an athlete who obviously is not prepared for that level of competition. This still happens at the USA T&F national level. Observe entry and qualification standards.

- Be positive but realistic about how long it takes to improve and reach national/world class. It has taken six years, on average, for the present crop of American 8000+ decathletes to reach that level. Score improvements are likely to be substantial in early years, then taper off. No one can add 300 points to his annual PR indefinitely. Physiology and the scoring tables do not work that way.

- Have patience. Be flexible.

- Decathlon coaches may find coaching a group very practical. Group allegiance can be generated, so that the athletes not only learn from but encourage one another.

- Collegiate coaches need to spell out team duties for decathletes *BEFORE* the season. This would include the number of decathlons to be contested, responsibilities in dual meets, and more. Under no circumstances should a coach ever ask a decathlete to handle relay duty immediately after a decathlon.

- Do not recruit a young athlete as a decathlete unless you are willing to train him as a decathlete first. Track-and-field athletes who are treated as secondary "decathletes" are unsuccessful.

- Don't be afraid to use assistant coaches. If you do, then attend as many sessions as possible conducted by the assistant coach. Make sure that coaches communicate and that workouts fit the overall scheme of the decathlete's training regime.

- Know the rules.

For Parents and Spouses

• Attend as many competitions as possible. From the athlete's standpoint, it is useful to show support for his efforts. But remember, there is a difference between parental support and parental pressure. Sometimes young athletes feel pressure BECAUSE their parents are in attendance. It's important for the athlete to know that parents will be supportive no matter what the final score or place.

• Encourage your child always to finish the decathlon. The one exception would be if he is injured.

• Don't brag about your child's accomplishments. The world-record holder's family could be seated directly behind you.

Courtesy of Iris Hensel

Spectators should get as close to the action as possible. Sitting on the infield during field events puts you in the middle of the action.

For Spectators

Keep score. It will give you something to do. Both the aforementioned IAAF Scoring Tables and *Big Green Book* will have short introductory sections on how to keep score. Bring paper and several pencils.

Have patience. The rules suggest (and athletes maintain) that there should be at least 30 minutes rest between events. Spectators end up viewing more rest than action—sort of like watching grass grow or paint dry.

If you intend to survive, here are a few suggestions concerning what to bring or do between events:

• Bring your breakfast.

• Bring a cushion for the creeping numbness in the hindquarters.

• Bring a dozen pencils and a scorecard.

• Bring your lunch.

• Learn the metric system.

• Bring a book or magazine.

• Listen to the announcer.

• Bring a radio or laptop computer (or both).

• Bring rain gear.

• Bring your dinner.

• Bring some spare change for a phone call explaining why you'll be late getting home.

• Be encouraging and noncritical. Get involved. Intend to survive. It takes stamina to be a decathlon spectator.

11

For Further Reading and Viewing

The young decathlete may be interested in additional books and articles on decathlon-related topics or be interested in visiting decathlon and decathlon-related Web sites. The author suggests the following:

BOOKS

Ancient Olympics

Young, D. (1984) *The Olympic Myth of Greek Amateur Athletics.* Chicago: Ares Publishers.

Modern Olympic Games

The Associated Press and Grolier. (1979) *Pursuit of Excellence, The Olympic Story.* New York: Franklin Watts.

Kamper, E. & Mallon, B. (1992) *The Golden Book of the Olympic Games.* Milan: Vallardi & Associates.

Mallon, B. & Buchanan, I, et al. (1984) *Quest for Gold: The Encyclopedia of American Olympians.* New York: Leisure Press.

Wallechinsky, D. (1991) *The Complete Book of the Olympics.* Boston: Little Brown.

Modern Track & Field History

Quercetani, R. (1990) *Athletics: A History of Modern Track and Field Athletics, 1860-1990.* Milan: Lallardi & Associates. (A new edition is scheduled for 2000.)

Decathlon History

Jenner, B. & Finch, P. (1977) *Decathlon Challenge: Bruce Jenner's Story.* Englewood Cliffs, NJ: Prentice Hall.

Johnson, D. with Becker, V. (1995) *Aim High: An Olympic Decathlete's Inspiring Story.* Grand Rapids, MI: Zondervan Publishing.

Newcombe, J. (1975) *The Best of the Athletic Boys.* Garden City, NY: Doubleday.

Rozin, S. (1983) *Daley Thompson: The Subject is Winning.* London: Stanley Paul & Company, Ltd.

Zarnowski, Frank (1989) *Decathlon: A Colorful History of Track's Most Challenging Event.* Champaign, IL: Leisure Press.

Decathlon Training

Doherty, K. (1985) *Track and Field Omnibook,* 4th ed, Mountain View, CA: Tafnews Press. (Chapter on decathlon training.)

Lease, D. (1990) *Combined Events.* (3rd ed.) Birmingham: British Amateur Athletic Board (BAAB).

O'Brien, D. (1998) *Dan O'Brien's Ultimate Workout*. New York: Hyperion Press.

Nutrition, Steroids, Injuries

Roy, S. & Irvin, R. (1983) *Sports Medicine: Prevention, Evaluation, Management & Rehabilitation*. Englewood Cliffs, NJ: Prentice Hall, Inc.

Wright, J.E. & Cowart, V.S. (1990) *Anabolic Steriods: Altered States*. Carmel, IN: Benchmark Press.

Goulart, F. (1985) *The Official Eating to Win Cookbook: Super Foods for Super Athletic Performance*. New York: Stein & Day.

Rules and Scoring Tables

IAAF Official Handbook, 2000/2001 (2000). Monte Carlo: International Amateur Athletic Federation (IAAF).

Editors of Track & Field News, (2000) *Big Green Book*. Mountain View, CA: Tafnews Press.

2000 Competition Rules for Athletics (2000). Indianapolis: USA Track & Field.

Scoring Tables for Men's and Women's Combined Events Competitions. (1995) Monte Carlo: International Amateur Athletic Federation.

Simmons, M. (ed.) (2000) *NCAA Track & Field/Cross Country Men's and Women's Rules*. Mission, KS: National Collegiate Athletic Association.

Records

van Kuijen, H. (ed.) (2001) *2000 Combined Events Annual*. de Bergen 66, 5706 RZ Helmond, Netherlands. (This is a must for serious multi-event fans.)

NEWSLETTERS

DECA Newsletter, c/o Frank Zarnowski, DECA, The Decathlon Association, Mount St. Mary's College, Emmitsburg, MD 21727 USA (8 issues per year). Now part of Web site: www.decathlonusa.org

WEB SITES

Web Sites Dealing Primarily with Decathlon:

DECA, The Decathlon Association Home Page. Set up in 2000, it is the premier American decathlon Web site offering sections on history, rules, annual schedules, records, book ordering, and publishing the 8x annually *DECA Newsletter.* It contains numerous links and an extensive overview of the sport.

www.decathlonusa.org

Estonian Decathlon Site. Titled *Decathlon 2000,* this site is in English, provides an excellent interface, and has up-to-date results page. Very professional. Emphasis on Estonia.

www.online.ee/~janeksal/index_english.htm

Team Decathlon UK. Offered by Richard Hunter, it serves as a clearing house for UK decathlons including StarMax. Popular.

www.vault.t/team-decathlon/

World's Greatest Athletes. Part of Azusa Pacific University T&F homepage, it offers terrific photos plus history and bios of great American decathletes, past and present. Presented by Kevin Reid, track coach at Azusa Pacific. Also links to a point calculator.

http://home.apu.edu/~kevreid/decathlon.html

Götzis Meeting Web site. A professionally constructed site telling viewer everything (results, entries, even travel arrangements and hotel accommodations) for the annual Götzis meeting in the Austrian Alps.

http://www2.vol.at/meeting-goetzis

Team Zehnkampf home page. Sponsored by Jeep and designed by German Olympian Frank Muller, this site updates viewer on news of the German decathlon team.

www.zehnkampfteam.de

The Austrian Decathlon. An extensive Web page maintained by ex-Austrian decathlete Robert Katzenbeisser, it has numerous links to other decathlon sites.

http://members.chello.at/katzenbeisser/

Swiss Decathlon Home Page. Information regarding decathlon in Switzerland.

www.decathlon.ch/

Combined Events of Canada. Information on Canadian meets. Often outdated.

http://www.speedandpower.com/combined/

Web Sites Dealing with Individual Decathletes

Official Site of Dan O'Brien. Visit the site of 1996 Olympic gold medalist Dan O'Brien and learn about him as a person, a decathlete, and an advocate for youth through the Dan O'Brien Youth Foundation.

http://www.danobrien.com/

Official Site of Tom Pappas. Visit the site of the 2000 national champion and Olympian Tom Pappas, who won the 2000 U.S. Olympic Trials.

www.DecaTom.com

Steve Fritz Fan Club. Site of fan club for American decathlete Steve Fritz who was 4th at 1996 Atlanta Olympic Games and 1997 national champion.

http://homepage.netspaceonline.com/~decafans/

Web Sites to Calculate Points

These sites allow you to type in your event results and receive an instant readout of your score. Especially helpful to the beginner. Also includes women's heptathlon count. They are in a variety of languages but are all easy to use.

Finnish: www.saunalahti.fi/~sut/eng/decathlon.html

English: http://espun.space.suri.edu/~anderson/jodi/
               DecaCalc.html

Japanese: http://ha1.seikyou.ne.jp.home/Naohiro.Nozaki/
               ayuu/tokuten6.htm

Related Track and Field Web Sites

IAAF: International Amateur Athletic Federation
http://www.iaaf.org

IOC: International Olympic Committee
http://www.olympic.org

USA T&F: USA Track & Field
www.usatf.org

Track & Field On Line:
www.trackonline.com

Track & Field News:
www.trackandfieldnews.com

TrackWire On Line:
www.trackwire.com

Run-Down Runner's Portal:
http://run-down.com

12

Decathlon Records

Outdoor

World
8994   THOMAS DVORAK/CZE   Prague, CZE   1999
(10.54 790 1678 204 48.08 13.73 4833 490 7232 4:37.20)

American
8891   DAN O'BRIEN/Reebok   Talence, FRA   1992
(10.43 808 1669 207 48.51 13.98 4856 500 6258 4:42.10)

World Junior
8397   THORSTEN VOSS/GDR   Erfut, GDR   1982
(10.76 766 1441 200 48.37 14.37 4176 480 6290 4:34.04)

American Junior
7658   KEITH ROBINSON/BYU   Houston, TX   1983
(11.02 674 1248 200 49.65 15.04 4422 430 5440 4:24.38)

High School
7359   CRAIG BRIGHAM/S Eugene HS Eugene, OR   1972
(10.9 673 1418 193 52.3 15.5 4416 443 6024 4:53.0)

Collegiate
8463   TOM PAPPAS/U of Tennessee   Tucson, AZ   1999
(10.75 752 1530 212 49.01 14.33 4866 500 6352 5:02.42)

Olympic Games
8847   DALEY THOMPSON/GBR Los Angeles, CA   1984
(10.44 801 1572 203 46.97 14.33 4656 500 6524 4:35.00)

One Hour
7897   ROBERT ZMELIK/TCH   Ostrava, CZE   1992
(10.89 764 1452 208 55.53 14.25 4192 480 6034 4:55.16)

Pentathlon
4282   BILL TOOMEY/USA-Striders London, GBR   1969
(758 6618 21.3 4453 4:20.3)

Indoor

Heptathlon
6476   DAN O'BRIEN/USA-Nike   Toronto, CAN   1993
(6.67 784 1602 213 7.85 520 2:57.96)

Pentathlon
4497   DAN O'BRIEN/USA-Reebok   Moscow, ID   1992
(track > 200m)   (7.88 735 1469 215 2:40.12)

Pentathlon
4478   STEVE FRITZ/USA-Accusplit Manhattan, KS 1995
(track = 200m)   (7.87 748 1613 206 2:45.32)

The Other Record Book

The decathlon event may be the most statistical, numerical event on the planet. Not only are there individual efforts that are recorded in minutes, seconds, tenths and even hundredths of seconds, but the field events marks are measured meters and centimeters, then transferred into to feet and inches. All these marks are scored, then added to previous totals, then compared, for place to other scores. It's all very numerical and only record keepers (and CPAs) could truly love the scoring aspect.

Well, for fun, here are some decathlon records you might not find elsewhere.

Career Records(with international implements/hurdles)

Most Career Meets

112	REX HARVEY, USA (WR, AR)	1965-86

Most Career Finishes

109	REX HARVEY, USA (WR, AR)	1965-86

Most Career Wins

31	VASILIY KUZNYETSOV, USSR (WR)	1953-64
30	KIP JANVRIN, USA (AR)	1983-2000

Most Consecutive Wins

13	BILL TOOMEY, USA (WR)	1968-70
12	BRUCE JENNER, USA	1974-76
12	DALEY THOMPSON, GBR	1980-86

(each had one dnf in streak)

Most Career Meets Over 8000 Points

34	CHRISTIAN PLAZIAT, FRA (WR) PR 8574	1985-96
26	TOMAS DVORAK, CZE PR 8994	1993-00
25	MIKE SMITH, CAN PR 8626	1988-98
24	KIP JANVRIN, USA (AR) PR 8462	1990-00
24	UWE FREIMUTH, GDR PR 8792	1981-88

Most Career Meets Over 7000 Points

61	KIP JANVRIN, USA (WR, AR) PR 8462	1986-00

Most Career Meets Over 6000 Points

97	REX HARVEY, USA (WR, AR) PR 7461	1969-86

Most Consecutive Finishes

41	KIP JANVRIN, USA (WR, AR) PR 8462 (including international + veterans meets)	1991-00
65	REX HARVEY, USA	1980-97

Most Career Points

REX HARVEY/USA (WR, AR)

Has scored nearly **one million career points**. The exact total depends on which tables one uses, since Harvey has competed for so long that his efforts have been scored on three sets of tables: 1962 IAAF, 1985 IAAF, WAVA. Suffice to say that he is far and away the all-time leading scorer in decathlon.

How Long Does It take?

One Hour Decathlon

The one hour decathlon was invented by Austrian decathlete, Dr. George Werthner. The rules are similar to the standard decathlon, but with 1500 meters starting within 60 minutes of the 100 meters. The event is usually run with two competitors side-by-side. This event has become very popular in Europe and is gaining popularity elsewhere. In 1994, Kip Janvrin won the most prestigious of the international one hour affairs, held in Robert Zmelik's hometown of Ostrava, Czech Republic. It may not be long before some highly fit decathlete scores over 8000 points in one hour!

7897   ROBERT ZMELIK/CZE (WR)   Ostrava   9/24/92
10.89 7.64m 14.52m 2.08m 55.53 14.25 41.92m 4.80m 60.34m 4:55.16

7774   SIMON POELMAN/NZL   Auckland   2/24/90
11.10 7.07m 15.75m 2.05m 55.51 15.19 44.64m 4.80m 58.38m 4:40.55

7591   STEVE FRITZ/Accsplit (AR)   Ostrava   9/24/93
11.15 7.12m 13.89m 1.95m 54.88 14.88 45.46m 4.90m 62.60m 5:03.37

7433   KIP JANVRIN/VISA   Ostrava   9/24/93
11.27 6.88m 13.42m 1.88m 48.86 15.28 46.08m 4.70m 58.38m 4:27.22

American Combinations

15,770   PAPPAS   Tom 8467, 2000 & Paul 7303, 1997

15,505   BRANHAM   Chris 8159, 1986 & Craig 7346, 1980

15,340   MCGORTY   Kevin 7990, 1992 & Dennis 7350, 1992

15,321   DIXON   Fred 8392, 1977 & Dave 6929, 1976

15,133   SAYRE   John 8381, 1985 & Tom 6752, 1978

15,043 STEBBINS Bob 7736, 1984 & Barry 7307, 1977

15,033 REID Bruce 7900, 1988 & Eric 7133, 1990

14,775 NOVACEK Jay 7762, 1984 & Jason 7013, 1985

14,735 MONDSCHEIN Brian 7810, 1980 & Mark 6925, 1976

14,604 BENNETT Mike 7753, 1994 & Dan 6851, 1995

14,591 KLEBAN Rick 7685, 1985 & Tom 6906, 1989

14,577 KLASSEN Steve 7390 1985 & Eric 7187 1993

14,229 BALCERSKI Ken 7179, 1985 & Bob 7050h, 1981

14,148 BARDALES Mauricio 8054, 1978 & Mario 6094, 1979

14,093 COLLINS Keith 7691, 1982 & Ken 6402, 1978

Brother-Brother-Brother Combination

22,968 PAPPSA, USA (WR,AR)
Tom 8467, 2000 & Paul 7303, 1997 &
Billy 7198, 2000

22,651 MCGORTY, USA
Kevin 7990, 1992 & Dennis 7350, 1992 &
Chris, 7311, 1980

Other Combinations

21,107 WERTHNER, AUT (ER)
George 8229, 1982 & Roland 7115, 1981 &
Ulrich 5763, 1988

20,688 KAHMA, FIN
Markus 7381, 1961 & Jörma 6964, 1963 &
Pennti 6551, 1965

20,688 BREDHOLT, NOR
Arild 7226, 1978 & Ivar 6825, 1978 &
Knut 6637, 1974

19,453   KRING, USA
         Kenny 7243, 1971 & Buddy 6127, 1977 &
         Timmy 6083, 1978

Brother-Brother-Brother-Brother

27,151   BREDHOLT, NOR (WR)
         Arild 7226, 1978 & Ivar 6825, 1978 &
         Knut 6637, 1974 & John 6463, 1962

Twins Record

16,425   RIZZI, GER (WR)   (16,469 on 1985 tables)
         Andreas 8369, 1983 & Thomas 8056, 1983

15,060   STEELE, USA (AR)
         Darrin 7892w, 1993 & Dan 7078, 1990

11,841   GOETZ, USA (the original Dan & Dave)
         Dave 5966, 1982 & Dan 5875, 1988

Father-Son Combination

15,406   MANDL, AUT (WR)
         Hörst 7760, 1969 & Jürgen 7646, 1986

15,085   RICHARDS, USA (AR)
         Bob 7381, 1954 & Tommy 7704, 1994

Other Combinations

15,275   STEEN, CAN
         Don 6860, 1958 & Dave 8415, 1988

15,067   HERMAN, USA
         Paul 8061, 1963 & Andrew 7007, 1993

14,883   SKRAMSTAD, NOR
         Knut-Henrik 6746, 1963 & Trond 8137, 1984

14,755   ERIKSSON, SWE
         Per 6730, 1947 & Thomas 8025, 1999

14,704   MONDSCHEIN, USA
         Irv 6894, 1949 & Brian 7810, 1980

14,548   MULKEY, USA
         Phil 8155, 1961 & Phil Jr 6393, 1977

14,451   JEWLEW, URA
         Wiktor 6772, 1949 & Wiktor, Jr 7679, 1972

14,042   FARMER, USA
         Dixon 6607, 1958 & Matt 7435, 1991

Father-Son-Son Combination

21,629   MONDSCHEIN, USA (WR)
         Irv 6894, 1949 & Brian 7810, 1980 &
         Mark 6925, 1974

20,756   WERTHNER, AUT (ER)
         Helmut 5412, 1953 & George 8229, 1982 &
         Roland 7115, 1981

20,647   MULKEY, USA
         Phil 8155, 1961 & Phil Jr 6393, 1977 &
         Tim 6099, 1974

20,637   HERMAN, USA
         Paul 8061, 1964 & Andrew 7007, 1993 &
         Robert 5569, 1989

19,946   HYTTEN, NOR
         Svein 6207, 1967 & Even 7406, 1991 &
         Iver 6333, 1987

Father-Son-Son-Son Combination

26,519   WERTHNER, AUT (WR)
          Helmut 5412,1953 & Georg 8229,1982 &
          Roland 7115, 1981 & Ulrich 5763, 1988

Timing Is Everything

Which decathlon records have lasted the longest and shortest length of time?

Who Has Held the World Record for the Longest Period of Time?

Believe it or not, it's a tie! 5116 days, held jointly by:

JIM THORPE/USA who set a world record at the Stockholm Olympic Games on July 15, 1912 and had it broken by Paavo Yrjola of Finland on July 18, 1926.

GLENN MORRIS/USA who first set a world record at the US Olympic Trials in Milwaukee, June 27, 1936 and reset a record at the Berlin Olympic games on August 8, 1936. His record was finally topped by Bob Mathias on June 30, 1950 in Tulare, California.

Which American Record Lasted the Longest Period of Time?

JIM THORPE/Carlisle set an American record at the Stockholm Olympic Games on July 15, 1912 and it lasted 5801 days (15 years, 323 days), finally broken by another native American, Fait Elkins/NYAC on June 3, 1928.

Which World Record Lasted the Shortest Period of Time?

BILL TOOMEY/Striders

On July 24, 1966, at an international meet at the Los Angeles Coliseum, Bill Toomey broke the existing world record (by scoring 8219 points) when he crossed the 1500 meters finish line in 4:20.3. However, when Russ Hodge crossed the line 20.1 seconds later (in 4:40.4) he totaled 8230 points and broke Toomey's record which had lasted all of 20.1 seconds.

AKILLES JARVINEN/FIN

A similar situation, ironically also at the Los Angeles Coliseum, occurred at the 1932 Olympic Games, August 6, 1932. When Jarvinen crossed the 1500-meter finish line in 4:47.0 he scored 8292.480 points, a new world record. He had only to wait for American Jim Bausch to finish to see if it would hold up. It did not. Bausch finished 30 seconds later (5:17.0) to reset the record at 8462.235 points.

13

Glossary

Like all sports, track and field has a language of its own. Knowing the language, using the correct terms, and designating the proper sports organizations will facilitate understanding for the decathlete, coach, official, parent, and spectator.

AAU The Amateur Athletic Union is a national organization that offers, among other sports, a Junior Olympic track-and-field program. It was formerly the national track federation. Its duties, in 1979, were turned over to The Athletic Congress (TAC), which formally changed its name to USA Track and Field in 1993.

Aerobic Sustained exercise, such as jogging or calisthenics, designed to stimulate and strengthen the heart without causing a loss of oxygen to the muscles. Literally, "with oxygen."

Anabolic Steroid A hormone, especially testosterone, that promotes growth of muscle tissue. Anabolic steroids have been banned by all track-and-field organizations which periodically test athletes for its presence. Positive tests result in bans.

Anaerobic Exercise, such as sprinting, designed to strengthen the heart while muscles lose oxygen. Literally, "in the absence of oxygen."

Automatic Timing Timing accomplished by an electronic device which times athletes to the 100th of a second. All major track meets now use automatic timing, which is necessary for world record approval.

Ballistic Sudden, very rapid, powerful movements.

Blocks Starting blocks, placed behind the starting line, are used by sprinters/hurdlers in races of 400 meters and under as an aid in starting.

Dan O'Brien Youth Foundation Founded in 1992 and named after the 1996 Olympic gold medalist, this foundation raises scholarship funds for needy youths, promotes citizenship, and offers a national high school decathlon championship.

DECA The Decathlon Association: a nonprofit organization whose purpose is to promote the decathlon and to publish and disseminate decathlon training, meet schedules, results, and information regarding records. Publishes the *DECA Newsletter* 8 times annually. The newsletter is now part of a Web site: www.decathlonusa.org.

Discus A circular disk, usually wooden with a metal rim, which is thrown. The seventh event of the decathlon.

Endurance Running
Long-distance running. Distances go to the marathon (26+ miles) and beyond. For decathletes, any training for the 1500 meters.

Fartlek
A running workout, used frequently by distance runners, wherein the speed is altered frequently. Interspersed with calisthenics. A Swedish term meaning "speed play."

Götzis
A small town in the Austrian Alps which annually conducts a popular international decathlon.

Heats
Sections of a running event. For races run in lanes, no fewer than three should start in any heat, and no more than the number of lanes.

Heptathlon
An indoor seven-event competition. For men the event consists of the 60m, long jump, shot put, and high jump on the first day and the 60m hurdles, pole vault, and 1000m run on the second day. The IAAF recognizes an official world record for this event. The women's heptathlon is the decathlon's female outdoor counterpart and consists of the 100m hurdles, high jump, long jump, and 200m on the first day, and the long jump, javelin, and 800m on the second day.

High Jump
The decathlon's fourth event wherein the competitor, using a running start and leaping off one foot, jumps for height over a crossbar.

Hurdles
A race with a series of ten 42-inch barriers (39 inches for high school athletes) over 110 meters. The decathlon's sixth event.

IAAF The International Amateur Athletic Federation is the governing body for track and field worldwide. The IAAF sets rules, provides scoring tables, and offers at two year intervals a world track and field championship. Home offices recently moved from London to Monte Carlo.

Imperial System An English system of measurement used primarily in the United States. The basic units of measurement are the inch, foot, yard, and mile. The decathlon does not use imperial distances.

Interval Training A training routine in which the athlete runs a series of specified distances for time with a designated rest period or "interval." Depending upon the speed of the runs, the workout can become anaerobic.

IOC The International Olympic Committee is responsible for conducting the Olympic Games.

Javelin A light spear, usually made of metal, which is thrown for distance. Approximately 8 feet in length with a cord handle and weighing 800 grams. The decathlon's penultimate event.

Junior A young athlete who does not turn age 20 in the current year. There are national and world junior championships.

Long Jump A leap for distance, into a sand landing pit, using a running start. Formerly called the "broad jump." The decathlon's second event.

Manual Timing Timing accomplished by hand (stop watch) to the 1/10th of a second. Digital watches that record times to the 1/100th of a second are a form of manual timing and results must be rounded up (*e.g.* 10.78 becomes 10.8).

Metric System An international system of measurement whose main (for track-and-field purposes) units of length are the meter (about 39 inches) and centimeter (about 0.4 inch). All decathlon events are measured in meters (*e.g.* 100 meters, 400 meters), and all field performances are also measured metrically.

NAIA The National Association of Intercollegiate Athletics is a national organization of small colleges and universities. The first national collegiate organization (1969) to offer a decathlon championship.

NCAA The National Collegiate Athletic Association is the governing body for most of America's colleges and universities. The NCAA provides rules for its members and offers a national decathlon championship.

Olympic Games A quadrennial celebration sponsored by the IOC wherein approximately 200 nations participate. The Olympic decathlon champion is normally cited as the "World's Greatest Athlete."

Pentathlon A five-event contest. Outdoors, the traditional pentathlon consists of the long jump, javelin, 200 meters, discus, and 1500 meters. Indoors the events normally are: 60m or 55m hurdles, long jump, shot put, high jump, and 1000 meters.

Pole Vault   The decathlon's eighth event wherein the athlete attempts to clear a crossbar with the use of a long (12- to 17-foot) vaulting pole. A foam rubber landing pit is necessary beyond the crossbar.

Power Training   Lifting weights, *e.g.*, barbells, in a prescribed manner for the purpose of enhancing strength. Useful mostly for the decathlon throwing events.

Shot Put   The third decathlon event in which a 16-pound (12-pound for high school athletes) metal ball is pushed or put for distance.

Sprints   A race at full speed for a short distance. The 100-meter sprint is the decathlon's initial event. Starting blocks are used, and the athlete responds to the commands and pistol of a starter.

Talence   A suburb of Bordeaux, France, which annually sponsors a major international decathlon called DecaStar.

USA T&F   USA Track & Field is America's national governing body for the sport. As with other track governing bodies, USA T&F offers rules, maintains records, and conducts a national championship for both junior and senior athletes and regional competitions.

USOC   The United States Olympic Committee sponsors the U.S. Olympic team every four years and conducts an annual domestic "Olympic Festival." The USOC also conducts national training centers in Colorado Springs, CO, and San Diego, CA.

WAVA   World Association of Veteran Athletes sponsors a world championships for masters age competitors, maintains veterans records, and sets rules for track and field in the veterans category.

Wind   For decathlon record purposes the aiding wind (tailwinds) in the 100 meters, long jump, and 110m hurdles cannot exceed 4 meters per second. The rule is 2 mps for open track-and-field events.

World Record   The highest total decathlon score officially approved by the IAAF. At the end of 2000, Thomas Dvorak's (Czech Republic) 8994 points stood as the world record. The world record has been broken 57 times since 1911.

14

Olympic and Decathlon Organizations

The organization of, and participation in, the Olympic Games requires the cooperation of a number of independent organizations.

The International Olympic Committee (IOC)

The IOC is responsible for determining where the Games will be held. It is also the obligation of its membership to uphold the principles of the Olympic Ideal and Philosophy beyond any personal, religious, national, or political interest. The IOC is responsible for sustaining the Olympic Movement.

The members of the IOC are individuals who act as the IOC's representatives in their respective countries, not as delegates of their countries within the IOC. The members meet once a year at the IOC Session. They retire at the end of the calendar year in which they turn 70 years old, unless they were elected before the opening of the 110th Session (December 11, 1999). In that case, they must retire at the age of 80. Members elected before 1966 are members for life. The IOC chooses and elects its members from among such persons as its nominations committee considers qualified. There are currently 113 members and 19 honorary members.

The International Olympic Committee's address is—

Chateau de Vidy, CH-1007
Lausanne, Switzerland
Tel: (41-21) 621-6111   Fax: (41-21) 621-6216
www.olympic.org

The National Olympic Committees

Olympic Committees have been created, with the design and objectives of the IOC, to prepare national teams to participate in the Olympic Games. Among the tasks of these committees is to promote the Olympic Movement and its principles at the national level.

The national committees work closely with the IOC in all aspects related to the Games. They are also responsible for applying the rules concerning eligibility of athletes for the Games. Today there are more than 150 national committees throughout the world.

The U.S. Olympic Committee's address is—

Olympic House
One Olympic Plaza
Colorado Springs, CO 80909-5760
Tel: (719) 632-5551   Fax: (719) 578-6216
www.olympic-usa.org

A Decathlete's Address Book

AAU Junior Olympics
c/o Don Kavades
National T&F Director
P.O. Box 1433
283 N. South Street
Porterville, CA 93250
Phone: 209-784-5485

ABC Radio's Vic Holchak
   Toll Free Track & Field
   Radio Reports
   Tel: 1-800-96-TRACK

American Track & Field
   Publisher-Larry Eder
   Shooting Star Media, Inc.
   16 E. Portola Avenue
   Los Altos, CA 94022
   Tel: 415-949-2072

Athletics Canada
   (Canadian T&F Federation)
   1600 James Naismith Drive
   Gloucester, Ontario K18 5N4
   Canada
   Tel: 613-748-5678

Dan O'Brien Youth Foundation
   c/o Doug Stiles
   P.O. Box 357
   Klamath Falls, OR 97601
   Tel: 503-884-2284

DECA, The Decathlon Association
   c/o Frank Zarnowski
   Mount St. Mary's College
   Emmitsburg, MD 21727
   Tel: 301-447-6122

High School Decathlons
   Brigham Young Invitational (held early May)
   c/o BYU PE Services, RB 112
   Provo, UT 84602
   Tel: 801-378-3994

Glendale Invitational (held early April)
c/o Carol Torrance
3412 W. Glenrose
Phoenix, AZ 85017
Tel: 602-336-2934

Great SouthWest (held late May)
Ed Hedges c/o Central High School
4525 N. Central
Phoenix, AZ 85012
Tel: 602-274-8100

New England High School (held early July)
John Buckley
14 Stagecoach Road
Hingham, MA 02043
Tel: 617-749-1308

Human Kinetics Publishers
(Publishers of "The Decathlon")
Box # 5076
Champaign, IL 61825
Tel: 1-800-747-4457

Hypo Bank Meeting
Late May in Götzis, Austria
Konrad Lerch, Meet Director
E-mail: Konrad.Lerch@vol.at

IAAF (International Amateur Athletic Federation)
17 Rue Princesse Florentine
Monte Carlo, MC 98000
Monaco
Tel: 33-9-330-7070

McFarland Publishing
Publishers of
The American Decathlete: A 20th Century Who's Who
Box # 611
Jefferson, NC 28640

NAIA (National Association of Intercollegiate Athletics)
6120 S. Yale Avenue, Suite 1450
Tulsa, OK 74136
Tel: 918-494-8828

National Masters News
Subscription Dept.
P.O. Box 5185
Pasadena, CA 91107
Tel: 818-577-7233

National T&F Hall of Fame Historical Research Library
c/o Rare Books Collections Librarian
Irwin Library
Butler University
4600 Sunset Avenue
Indianapolis, IN 46208
Tel: 317-283-9265

NCAA (National Collegiate Athletic Association)
700 W. Washington Ave.
P.O. Box # 6222
Indianapolis, IN 46206-6222
Tel: 317-917-6222
Fax: 317-917-6888

NFSHSAA (Nat. Fed. of State H.S. Athletic Assns.)
P.O. Box 206206
Kansas City, MO 64195
Tel: 816-464-5400

NJCAA (National Junior College Athletic Association)
P.O. Box 7305
Colorado Springs, CO 80933
Tel: 719-590-9788

T&FN (Track & Field News)
2570 El Camino Real, Suite 606
Mountain View, CA 94040
Tel: 415-948-8188

USA Track & Field (USA T&F)
Box # 120
One RCA Dome, Suite 140
Indianapolis, IN 46225
Tel: 317-261-0500

USA T&F, Chair of Decathlon Olympic Development
Committee
Scott Hall
Track Coach
University of Northern Colorado
2423 29th Avenue
Greeley, CO 80634
Tel: 970-330-6028

USDTF (U.S. Decathlon Team Foundation)
Chairman: Tom Slattery
460 Anchorage Drive
Nokomis, FL 34275
Tel: 941-488-4542
E-mail: tslattery@dellnet.com

Veteran/Masters Decathlons
Rex Harvey
160 Chatham Way
Mayfield Heights, OH 44124
Tel: 216-446-0559

WAVA (World Association of Veteran Athletes)
Barbara Kousky
5319 Donald Street
Eugene, OR 97405
Home: 503-687-8787
Office: 503-687-1989
Fax: 503-687-1016

15

2000 Olympic Games

With American record holder Dan O'Brien sidelined by a foot injury, U.S. hopes for a 2000 gold medal rested mainly on Chris Huffins. The 30-year-old American managed a bronze, but top honors in the decathlon at Sydney went to Erki Nool of Estonia and Roman Sebrle of the Czech Republic.

Preparing for Sydney

For Huffins, the fast track to Sydney began with the run-up to Atlanta.

Every athlete has the ability to get hot on occasion. But few have competitions like Chris Huffins did in the decathlon at the 1996 Olympic Trials. Most expected him to make the team, but who expected he would do it with a personal best in all five events on day one? He opened with a 10.22 in the 100 meters, faster than any decathlete had ever gone. That's hot.

On day two, Huffins cooled down to the incendiary level, only grabbing two more PRs on his way to an overall score of 8546, a lifetime best by nearly 200 points.

"I think that an Olympic year is always what you make of it," said Huffins, who followed up his third in the Trials with a tenth-place finish in the Atlanta Games. "To be completely honest, I was as pleased with the way I competed in the Games as I was in the outcome of the Trials. I had some misfortune in the long jump, I had two fouls that were the difference between being in the top five and being tenth. Knowing that things were going to continue to be uphill, I just continued to fight. I had the best next eight events I've had."

In 1991, the year that Dan O'Brien won his first World Championship in the decathlon, Huffins sat in the stands at Berkeley's Edwards Stadium with a broken toe, watching his Cal teammates train. He told Scott Horner of the *Indianapolis Star*, "I was sitting there saying 'I can do this and I can do that.' So my coach said, 'Go out and prove it.'"

The coach, Ed Miller, had won the 1976 NCAA decathlon. He wasn't completely joking when he challenged the sprinter/long jumper to the big event. He knew Huffins had some basic throwing skills. And as he told Horner, "Some people have the skills but can't stay on the field for eight or ten hours. But he's a track-and-field junkie."

A year later, Huffins finally gave it a shot, scoring 7531 in Tempe, AZ. "I thought I did horribly," he said. Miller thought otherwise. Huffins added 354 points on his next outing, and that took him to the Olympic Trials. In New Orleans, he stood second in the standings after the first day, then plummeted to 15th at the end. In 1993, Huffins won the NCAAs in 8007. "It almost came too easy," said Miller.

Huffins, like a typical Hoosier, started out playing basketball. His mother allowed him one sport in high school, and it was not until his junior year that he could persuade her to let him try sprinting and long jumping. He learned the trade from a local masters athlete named Donna Green—she had once been a state champion long jumper herself. He graduated a 23-foot, 6.5-inch jumper and headed to Purdue for two years. He made it to the NCAAs as a Boilermaker but failed to distinguish himself. After his sophomore year he transferred to Cal.

Up to 1993, Huffins looked like a great prospect in the decathlon. Then he spent most of 1994 trying to recover from an injury.

In 1995, Huffins showed up at Nationals with a 7940 under his belt. After day one, he again found himself in second place. This time, he held on—and took some chances. In the vault, the chanciest event of the decathlon, Huffins waited until the bar was raised above his existing PR before he took his first attempt. The gamble wasn't what it had seemed, said Huffins. He had been clearing higher heights all season in practice. "I would not have done that if my coach weren't 100% confident that I would be able to make it," he said.

It all paid off. He scored 8351 for second and a trip to the World Championships in Sweden. Many hailed the meet as a major breakthrough. Huffins took a different view. "To be honest, I didn't think that 1995 was a breakthrough," he said. "I think it was a return to the track that I'd been on before I got injured. I thought I was going to put up a bigger score. I'm trying to catch up to where I think I should be."

At the Worlds, Huffins scored 8193 for eighth, "I would have liked to be in the top five, but I did the best job I possibly could," he said. For his efforts, he ranked number eight in the world.

A voracious trainer, Huffins typically put in 60 hours a week at the track. When he wasn't at the track, he spent his spare time reviewing his collection of hundreds of track videos. "It's a complete and total commitment for me," he said. "If you compete for a living there's no such thing as being too competitive. I don't worry about being able to turn it off. My career is intense, but when I'm done, 2001 or whenever I decide to stop running, I'll be done. Then a game of cards will be a game of cards with friends. It won't be an extension of my personality. My personality now, if I'm playing a game of tiddlywinks with my grandmother, I'm still trying to take her to the mat."

For Huffins, a driven man in every sense, there was no complacency: "You've got to forget what you did, or else you'll never get to do what you want to do."

The 2000 Competition

Huffins became the American hopeful to win the decathlon when Dan O'Brien, gold medal winner at the Atlanta Games in 1996, withdrew from Olympic contention just two days before the start of the U.S. Trials. O'Brien dropped from the Trials due to a partial tissue tear in his left foot, which he suffered while practicing the high jump.

Huffins, the two-time defending U.S. champion and winner of the bronze medal in the 1999 World Championships, would still have to face Tomas Dvorak of the Czech Republic and Great Britain's Dean Macey, who had taken silver at the World Championships. Dvorak, who surpassed O'Brien's world record with 8994 points in 1999, was considered the favorite to win gold going into the Games.

100 Meters

The two-day, ten-event competition began, despite poor weather conditions, with runners taking to a wet track to sprint the 100 meters. The weather may have hampered performances, as none of the 38 runners had a personal record.

Huffins, showing his strength as a sprinter, won the event with a time of 10.48. Nool placed second, coming in at 10.68. Dvorak, suffering from a knee injury and a torn stomach muscle, ran the 100 in 10.91, one of his slowest times in five years.

Long Jump

Dvorak continued to struggle, managing only 7.50 meters in the long jump. Nool again took second, with a jump of 7.76 meters. But it was Macey, with a personal best, who won the event by one thousandth of a meter. Huffins placed third with 7.71 meters but still led the competition in overall points.

Shot Put

Although Nool set a personal record in the shot put with 15.11 meters, it was Dvorak who won the event with a 15.91-meter round. This was the first win of the competition for Dvorak—a far cry from his world record performance at the European Cup in 1999, where he set personal bests in five of the ten events.

High Jump

U.S. team member Tom Pappas gave a spectacular performance in the high jump to win the event. His personal record of 2.21 meters, equaling the ninth-best high jump in decathlon history, put him second behind Huffins in overall points. With the two Americans in the top spots after this event, it looked as though the U.S. might take two medals in the decathlon.

400 Meters

Macey, who had suffered a hamstring injury earlier in the season, set a personal best in the 400 meters with 46.41 seconds, running the seventh-best time in decathlon history. His win in the event placed him second behind Huffins, who maintained his lead in overall points. Dvorak finished last in his heat with a time of 49.11 seconds, forcing him to give up any hope of a gold medal.

110-Meter Hurdles

The Americans Huffins and Pappas nabbed second and third in the 110-meter hurdles. But it was Roman Sebrle of the Czech Republic who won the event, catapulting him into medal contention.

Discus

Controversy surrounded the discus event when Nool, a strong contender for the gold, fouled on his first two throws. On his third attempt, he initially earned the white flag and a mark of 43.66 meters. The red flag indicating a third foul was raised, however, when officials reviewed television replays and determined that Nool's foot was outside the circle.

Nool appealed the decision, and it was later judged that his heel was inside the circle. A protest lodged by Great Britain, the U.S., and the Czech Republic was dismissed, and the throw was reinstated. The reversal of the decision, which had dropped him to 24th in the standings and smashed all his hopes for a medal, meant that Nool was now third overall and still in the running for gold.

Pole Vault

Nool, having cleared 5.50 meters at meets earlier in the season, was in a perfect position to win the pole vault event and secure the gold. He easily cleared 5.00 meters, but then decided to pass on 5.10 and go directly to 5.20, which eluded him on all three attempts. That left the medal competition wide open.

Javelin

On day two of the decathlon competition, with just two events remaining, Huffins still held the overall lead. It was a lead he had maintained through every event since the 100 meters. The question was whether the lead would prove big enough to carry him through two of his weaker events, the javelin and the 1500 meters. The answer was—no.

Dvorak, who holds the world record in the javelin, won the event with a mark of 69.94 meters. His win would allow him to run in the final 1500-meter race and finish the competition. Nool's fourth-place showing in the event (65.82 meters), combined with Huffins' disappointing throw of 56.62 meters, gave Nool second place in the overall standings, just 14 points behind Huffins. Holding down third place was Sebrle, 40 points behind Nool.

1500 Meters

In a statement of will befitting the most grueling venue in track and field, American Kip Janvrin, the oldest athlete in history to compete in a modern Olympic decathlon, ran an impressive 4:17.81 to win the 1500 meters. Despite a personal best of 4:38.71, Huffins could not hold onto his lead. In a dramatic finish, Nool and Sebrle were forced to run their own personal bests in order to edge out Huffins for gold and silver, respectively. Macey could not overtake the American, despite his own personal record of 4:33.45, and Huffins, who had held the lead through nine of ten events, captured the bronze. Nool's winning score was 8641, followed by Sebrle (8606), Huffins (8595), and Macey (8567).

Pappas finished in fifth place with 8425. Dvorak, the world record holder, who had been favored to win prior to the Games and had set his sights on the elusive 9000 mark, finished a disappointing sixth with 8385. Despite his heroic performance in the 1500 meters, Janvrin finished no better than 21st, with an overall score of 7726.

About the Author

Frank Zarnowski, Ph.D., is a professor of economics at Mt. St. Mary's College, Emmitsburg, MD. Dr. Zarnowski has authored numerous books on the subject of the decathlon, including *Olympic Glory Denied* (Griffin Publishing Group). He has also served as television commentator and public address announcer for decathlon competitions. He has been a longtime fan of the sport.